Wealth Over Riches

Escaping the Paycheck to Paycheck Cycle

Will Thomas

To: Ashley

I hope the book blesses you!

www.IamWillThomas.com

© 2019 Will Thomas

All rights reserved. No portion of this book may be reproduced in any form without permission from the publisher, except as permitted by U.S. copyright law. For permissions contact:

info@iamwillthomas.com

Cover by Eric Johnson

Paperback ISBN: 978-0-578-61751-0

Imprint: Thomas Publishing

Acknowledgements

I would like to start off first by thanking my lovely wife, Tiffany Thomas. Thank you for all of the love, help, and patience you provided me during the process of writing the book. You were onboard from the very beginning and I truly appreciate your feedback and involvement in the process of creating this book.

Next, I would like to thank my team of initial editors and reviewers: Tiara Davis, Rodney Hopper, Michael Washington, and Arles Wood. You guys were quick to jump into the process when asked upon. You guys are apart of the blessing this book will bring to others.

I would like to thank my final editor and high school English teacher, Miss McCullough. Truly, I appreciate the time taken out of your busy schedule to provide the final touches to this project. There is no way I would have been able to produce this book without you being in my life to challenge me in high school. You converted a math guy into an author!

Lastly, I would like to thank my illustrator, graphic designer, and fraternity brother Eric Johnson. Thank you for providing the initial concept for the book via the book cover, and for all the work you do for me.

"An investment in knowledge pays the best interest."

- Benjamin Franklin

Introduction

When you die, do you want to leave a check or bill to your beneficiaries? Do you want to build wealth and pass it on to your family? Or do you want to bury your riches in a tomb like a pharaoh? This is a simple question that determines what you really want out of life for your finances.

Many of you have probably never thought that far ahead. You are too busy trying to escape bill collectors or to figure out how to make it until next month. The paycheck-to-paycheck cycle is the number one threat to never obtaining and sustaining wealth. They are actually on two total opposite financial spectrums. It is a no brainer; if you are currently in the paycheck-to-paycheck cycle that you cannot foresee the ability to accumulate wealth.

Many of you may even think you are not living paycheck-to-paycheck. Can you afford to lose your job or be without income for three months? Do you have credit bills besides your day to day cost of living? If you answered yes to these questions, I want to inform you that you are actually living paycheck-to-paycheck, regardless of your current income.

The key is that you do not have to continue to live your life paycheck-to-paycheck. You have already acknowledged that you can do better by reading this book. For those who have not yet, hopefully by the end of this book you will gain the motivation to do better.

Thank you for investing in yourself by purchasing this book. Thank you for acknowledging that you can always use additional knowledge on how to manage your personal finances. My goal for this book is for you to apply the knowledge gained to escape the paycheck-to-paycheck cycle and to save over one thousand times the price of this book.

The purpose for writing this book is to give you a clear and defining perspective on how to manage your money. There are millions of personal finance and self-help books, but few rarely give true examples of personal mistakes made. So many authors are selling a dream after they went bankrupt. Unlike those authors, this book connects with you on a personal level. While writing this book, I wanted to be vulnerable and share with you some of my own personal financial struggles and the mistakes. At the end of the book, I will share my personal finance goals along with my blueprint to financial freedom.

I dedicated the time and effort to writing this book solely for YOU! This book is for the person working multiple jobs, but still cannot escape your financial burdens. It is for the high school student with dreams and aspirations to be a millionaire one day. It is for the recent college graduate with thousands of dollars in student debt while juggling being an adult for the first time in their lives. This book is for the person who every month seems to spend more than they actually have. This book is for everyone who did not grow up wealthy and never had real financial conversations with your family. This book is for you, solely on the fact you are investing the time to read the book.

I hope that my insight and experience with my own personal finances will be beneficial to you, and help you reach your financial goals. I am a huge fan of continual growth, and I hope this book in some way will motivate you to continue to learn about how to better manage your finances. This is your starter book to motivate you to read additional finance books or listen to other finance outlets to gain more knowledge that will help you reach your financial goals. One thing I have learned is that no matter how successful you are with your personal finances, there is always something new to learn from a fresh perspective.

My passion for seeing others reach their goals comes from my own continual growth in my personal finances. This book will include answers to questions my friends have constantly asked me over the years. It will also include success stories as well as mistakes that I have made with my own finances. Being completely honest, I am not a finance guru. I have a Bachelor's degree in Computer Science and a Master's degree in Information Technology. With that being said, my friends and family must think I am a financial guru with all the questions that I constantly receive.

My knowledge of how to handle my finances was at times gained by trial and error, and can be painted as more of a roller coaster than a smooth race up hill. But just like you are taking the time to read this book, I invested countless hours reading personal finance books, listening to podcasts, and reading financial blogs to educate myself to become more financially sound. Remember, you can either lose a lot of money by trusting your own knowledge and taking the trial and error approach; or you can tap into other's perspectives and gain new knowledge that will help you earn exponentially more than the cost of this book.

If you are already experienced with your personal finances or have read other books, then you definitely know that there are multiple viewpoints on how you should manage your money. There are books on multiple topics from how to become financially free to books on how to get out of debt and become rich. If you are in debt, you already know that getting out of debt is HARD. Never let a book, blog, or social media influencer make you feel that it just happens overnight. It takes extreme sacrifice along with adjusting your mindset on your finances in order for you to really overcome debt and build wealth. Most debt is not accumulated in one day; so do not expect it to disappear overnight.

This book will give you my perspective on how to manage your money. My perspective integrates various financial viewpoints. The first book that comes to mind is Dave Ramsey's Total Money Makeover. You will see that a lot of my ideas and viewpoints align with Dave's viewpoints. In Total Money Makeover, Ramsey gives you a multi-step plan to financial freedom (Ramsey, 2007). Ramsey is a huge believer in a credit free, debt free life. He gives a solid guide on how to get out of debt and stay out of debt if you are willing to make the necessary sacrifices. This book will have a similar philosophy, but will also allow for more personal freedom during your journey.

Another book that I will refer is Scott Trench's *Set for Life*. Like Ramsey, Trench believes in extreme sacrifice to reach your financial goals (Trench, 2017). In *Set for Life*, he wrote about how to build your wealth and income to a point where you can leave a traditional hourly job; Trench's book begins in a similar manner as this one does. He is a true believer in building wealth via real estate, and gives really good advice for people who have the will and flexibility to follow his plan.

A third book is JL Collins's book, *The Simple Path to Wealth*. Collins's book focuses on how to invest your money (Collins, 2016). In this book, I reference *The Simple Path to Wealth* a lot in the section on Investments for Wealth Building. I highly recommend reading all three books upon finishing this one. One common viewpoint, in all of the mentioned books, is that reaching your financial goals will take a lot of sacrifice. When I say a lot, I MEAN a lot of sacrifice. Before you continue to read, you have to determine how badly you want your personal finances to change.

I hope that through this book, I can help encourage you to take more time to plan your finances. I hope I can help you understand how to enjoy life while sacrificing to reach your goals. I hope I can help you to create a financial goal list, put a solid plan in place to reach those goals, and then motivate you to achieve every goal on that list. By the end of this book, I hope you are motivated and inspired to hit the ground running toward your financial goals.

Chapter 1 - Changing Current Financial Habits

Why do we spend so much money?

Nobody wants to admit it, but we all struggle from time to time with our spending. If that were not the case, people in the United States would not be in a total of $1 trillion dollars in total credit card debt. From the emotional trips to the mall to eating out daily, we have a huge problem with spending money. Statistics say that only 1 in 3 households actually budgets their expenses. So I am just going to assume that you are in the non-budget category. For those that actually budget your money, I want you to literally pat yourself on the back, because you are already ahead of most of the people that you know.

For those who do not budget, do not feel ashamed. As you can see from the statistics, you are in the majority. I already know that by not having a budget makes it extremely hard to manage your money, but do not feel embarrassed because those, like myself with budgets still struggle with our spending. That is mainly because the budget is only a plan. The budget helps plan our money for the week, month, or year, but it does not control the person spending the money.

Now, here is the first gem that I am going to drop in this book. In order to truly become financially stable, you have to become less of a consumer and more of a saver. If you are or are not taking notes, please write that sentence down. That is the base of how to truly begin the race towards financial peace and freedom. You have to embrace the mindset of a saver. Today, most of us are daily consumers. We have to buy food, pay bills, and so on. Daily, we have to reach in our wallets and swipe our cards, because nothing in this world is truly free. You are not alone. Believe me the mindset change from primarily being a consumer to a saver is extremely hard.

Daily, we are being coerced into spending our hard earned money. From television and radio commercials, ads on websites, and even billboards while driving to work, we are constantly being pitched different products that we "need" in our lives. Especially in the hip hop culture, we see millionaires buying the things they could never afford before they made it big. We, as a culture, follow the same steps. As we gain more and more money, we tend to spend more and more money. It's the capitalist way! You would not be considered American if you did not spend money to show how much you actually make.

It makes total sense does it not? Why work forty plus hours a week just to sit in the house and watch YouTube videos all weekend? Especially when you get on social media and see your friends out drinking or at a concert. We are programmed from elementary school to follow a path that will help us gain more money so we can get everything we ever wanted and could not afford at a young age.

Until you truly understand how we are persuaded to spend our hard working money, you will continue to struggle with your spending. There are reasons why food commercials pop up on late night television. It has been hours since our last meal, and restaurants do not have steady customers at later hours. We are literally guinea pigs for marketing firms to help their clients reach higher and higher profits. We literally are persuaded, on a daily basis, to buy everything that we use or consume constantly. Honest moment, I persuaded you via marketing myself to get you to buy this book. Whether I know you personally or used a marketing pitch to get you to buy the book, I had to market the book to get you to read it. Marketing is an important aspect of our economy. Otherwise, we would overlook the majority of the things we purchase.

We are too busy in our daily lives spending most of our time earning money to pay for all these things "that we need" instead of researching and investigating everything that we will eventually spend our dollars on. We do not have enough time in a day to do so. We actually need these marketing firms to present us with the best options for the various products we buy.

Seriously, for the drinkers reading this, would you ever drink Ciroc if Diddy did not market it in all his music videos? Would you even know what Taco Bell had on its seasonal menu if they did not have the food commercials? Would you even know who Barack Obama was if there were not people who invested in commercials to make him mainstream way before he decided to run for President? I can honestly answer no to all three questions.

Our money issues are not with the marketing firms. We already know we actually need them in our lives. Our true issue is that we are weak minded, at times, and allow these firms to persuade us to spend every last cent in our bank accounts. Our true issue is ourselves. We spend so much money, because we cannot control ourselves when presented with the opportunity to buy the latest and greatest products.

If the prior paragraph were not true, there would be no way Apple could charge us over $1,000 for a phone. The craziest part of it all, people are still lining up to be the first person to get it. That is truly astonishing that, not only do we have to buy the phone, but also we have to be the first one with the phone. Honestly, what benefit, other than showing it off to others, does having the phone first bring us? There are no benefits outside of social acceptance.

So, maybe, we have identified that is the true underlying issue. We spend so much money to show off to others that we are making it in life. We are trying to show that we can afford designer clothes and foreign cars. We do not spend a lot of money just to spend it, but rather with the alternative motive to show off what we are actually spending it on!

True needs vs. wants

As previously mentioned, a lot of us are wasting money just trying to prove our social status. We buy big houses, new cars, new phones, and etc.; just to be able to say, hey I am working hard and can live like a boss. A lot of our habits are often driven by culture, but we play into it ourselves as well. If you do not think so, look at the pictures on your social media accounts from over five plus years ago. You will quickly think about how immature you were posting pictures of items you no longer have or things you will have to take time off work just to find in your closet. The desire to be accepted is the American way, and has been programmed into our minds since birth.

I am here to help you avoid this downfall. In order to do so, we have to first understand the difference between a need and a want. I am sure that you probably have or are on your way to graduating from high school so you know the difference, but have you ever listed your needs and wants from a financial perspective? That is basically what a budget is. It is a financial listing of your needs and wants for a given income that you can spend.

Just take a second to really digest it. Your budget does not have to be inputted into some super cool new application like Mint or some macro infused spreadsheet on Excel. It can be a simple list made every paycheck of what you have to pay versus what you would really like to buy. The key to truly becoming a successful budgeter is to understand that your needs must always come before your wants. If you did not catch that, you missed another gem worth writing down regardless of how simple it seems. My needs are more important than my wants, and I have to apply that mentality daily in order for me to become successful at my financial goals.

So what are your true financial needs? For the non-budgeter, you are probably thinking about food, clothes, and occasional outings with friends. Although food is a need, those others are considered wants when you want to become successful at your financial goals. A true need is something in your budget that you have no choice but to pay for or to suffer financially. Now let us explore some financial needs that everyone will be in need of. Your mortgage or rent is a need. You have to live somewhere or risk the chance of being homeless. Once you have a place to stay, the next need is energy or gas depending on your living situation. You will have to power your living space and keep it at a comfortable temperature to survive. Another need associated with living space is your water bill. These include other utility bills associated with your living space. All utility bills are needs because you have to pay them as part of managing your living space or else you will risk your credit score dropping for late payments.

Another need to consider is transportation money. Note, I did not say car payment. I said transportation money. This money will be used to get from your living space to your place of employment. This can be public transportation fare or gas money if you have a car. If you have a car, you are truly blessed. We will discuss why car payments are not a need later in the book.

If you are wise enough to make money on the Internet, that too now becomes a need. If you only use the Internet at home for playing video games online and to stream movies and television shows, the Internet is no longer a need. If you are making money via the Internet, it is definitely a need and falls in a similar category as transportation money. This is money used to allow you to bring in additional revenue. Just look at it as one of your first initial investments. You are investing in yourself to make more money and truly are in control of the return on investment.

Now, back to owning a car. If you live in certain states that require car insurance that now becomes a need. You have no choice but to pay for it or you will suffer more financially by not having it. With that being said, please consider this a need as well. The other important need is food. We all have to survive in order to actually work and food fuels us to be able to go make our money. It is definitely a need. Other than the needs listed above, unless you can justify financial liability, everything else you spend money on are wants.

I know you are thinking now, what is he talking about. A couple things that come to mind that you definitely will associate as needs are clothes and childcare if you have kids. Yes, these might seem as though they are required to live a proper life, but are they needs in your weekly or monthly budget? Childcare honestly can swing both ways. If both parents work and individually bring in more money than childcare costs, childcare is a need. Likewise for the single parent who has no choice but to pay for childcare, childcare is definitely a need. However, for those who do not make more individually than childcare cost in a two-parent home, childcare then becomes a want based on your desire to work instead of staying at home with the children.

Now on the topic of clothes, yes we need them; but do we need to buy new clothes every month? Some people will argue yes, but honestly we do not. Clothes tend to be one of the biggest things that the average person overspends their money on. Remember this book is about becoming better with your personal finances, and understanding the behaviors that have prohibited our current financial success. For those with true clothing needs that outweigh your income, we will discuss ways to help alleviate your burdens later in the book.

Now that we covered needs, what are wants? Wants are things we have control over or we just desire them in our lives. Wants are what keep us from really achieving our financial goals. We have clever brains that think of some amazing things so the list of wants is never ending; but as you are starting to understand about why we spend so much and how we can gain the power of self control, you will limit your "wants" list.

When saying wants are things we have some control over, we really understand that we have control over what type of products we actually buy. For example, you have about 5-10 options of soap you can buy from the local store. Just because you can afford it does not mean you should buy the most expensive soap in the store. You have total control on whether you will be financially sound in choosing a soap brand. Do you have to buy the store brand soap? No, but you have a choice to determine if you want to be persuaded into buying the higher brand or you can be financially sound and buy a reasonably priced soap.

That type of decision-making should be made on almost all your wants. From the clothes you buy, to the car you drive, you have total control on what is a financially sound purchase versus one that will hurt you financially in the long run. For those of you reading this who are in major debt, think about it. That debt did not start overnight. You did not blow $30,000 at the casino, or maybe you did. But for most people, it was an accumulation of multiple poorly made decisions that led to the amount of debt you have. One crazy thing is that the same type of decision-making can be applied to some of our needs as well.

The main reason why the list of true needs is so small is because we truly have a lot of control on how we spend our money. I know at the end of the month it definitely does not feel that way after paying all of your bills. But if you took a second to look through your card statements and reevaluated your budget, you will quickly see how those nights eating out and random trips to the mall were completely under your control.

True needs are things we have to pay for to prevent from suffering financially. Things we want to make sure are covered first in the budget. So many people are living paycheck-to-paycheck, because they lack the understanding of what a true need is. Also, they do not practice good financial decision making on purchasing their needs and wants. The very first step to truly break the cycle of paycheck-to-paycheck is to understand our needs come first and our wants are totally under our control.

Finding your true passions of spending

Last section, we covered true needs versus wants, and now we have the foundation for formatting our budget. This budget will be our rulebook to measure how financially sound we really are. Again, we have to first understand what our true needs are and add them to the budget first. Once we have our needs in place, then hopefully we have some extra money for our wants.

Since you took the time to read this, I am going to assume that your first want is to break the paycheck-to-paycheck cycle. By committing to that want, you will have to sacrifice most of the wants we talked about in the previous section. The next thing after needs on your budget should reflect this desire in your life. To accomplish this, your budget after your needs should be focused on savings and debt reduction, which we will cover in more detail later on. Put a placeholder in your budget for that. Make sure you type or write it in bold.

After establishing the placeholders for relieving your paycheck-to-paycheck cycle, you now have a small bucket to purchase your wants. Make sure you really plan out those things that you know you want on a monthly cycle, or you will stress out without them. For females, those can be a monthly hair, manicure, or pedicure appointment. For males, that can be your haircut twice a month. The list of wants can go on and on.

With that in mind, I want to focus this section on those wants that are so important that you actually contemplate on putting them above the placeholder section for savings and debt reduction. We will call these desired wants. Desired wants are things that will give you satisfaction and make you proud of your hard-earned money. For some people, a desired want is a fancy car. For others, desired wants are their clothes or shoes. If you give tithes to church or donate to a certain organization, that donation would be considered a desired want or to some a need or necessity.

For me, traveling is definitely a desired want. As expensive as traveling the world can be, no amount of money in the bank can fulfill the feeling I have when I am on vacation. Desired wants should make you feel the same way. These are things that make waking up early on a Monday morning worth it. Desired wants should be really important to you, because these are the wants that you will never regret spending your money on no matter the circumstance. You never want to regret purchasing your desired wants, and you should actually look forward to the next time you can actually purchase them again.

Most financial books, including the two previously covered, do not put a focus on what I call desired wants. They preach strict financial principles until you reach your financial goals. Unlike them, I truly believe in balance. Life is too short. You can save every dollar after paying your needs, but never really enjoy your hard-earned money before you die. Balance is key to true happiness, and you should be chasing happiness over riches. The point of breaking the paycheck-to-paycheck cycle is pure happiness and a less stressful life, so I want to be sure that you have the balance in your budget to reach those goals.

Always re-evaluate your finances

For the readers who actually do budget, but still have trouble understanding why you struggle with your finances; one of the main reasons is that you do not re-evaluate your budget on a periodic timeline. As we all know, people change very often, so if people change their finances definitely will change. From having kids to purchasing a house, life happens to the best of us, and it is a great practice to always take time to re-evaluate our finances. You do not have to wait until major life changes happen to readjust your budget. You should have a weekly, monthly, yearly, five year, and ten year plan to your budget with goals that align with your plan.

With that in mind, it would be a great idea to take time weekly, monthly, and yearly to re-evaluate your financial life. One year, your desired want may be to travel. The next year, your desired want could be to go back to school and be able to finance it yourself. With constant change in your life, the best thing to do is to constantly re-evaluate and adjust your budget.

It does not take much effort from time to time to look at your budget. Periodically take the time to write down your current true needs, desired wants, and wants, and then compare that list to your previous budget. If anything does not add up, adjust the budget to make sure the list is properly accounted for. This is a cycle you will get accustomed to, and every time you go to re-evaluate your finances, it will become easier and easier.

Another way to help speed up the time it takes to re-evaluate your budget is to forecast your budget for your long-term goals. In my current budget spreadsheet, I have several tabs. I have my main budget tab that accounts for my income and spending for the month. I have another tab that is purely used to forecast my short and long term spending. The next tab is used to verify my personal spending for the month on my credit card. The total from that tab is on the main budget tab but this tab gives me a personal sub-budget to manage for my personal monthly spending. The next tab calculates my salary and bonuses based on the information I know, and projections of what my raise and bonus could be in the future. Will these forecast be exactly right every time, NO! But there is nothing wrong with trying to plan ahead. We already talked about it before. Yes, life will happen, but can you totally be financially wise if you do not think financially forward? As you start to plan your short and long-term financial goals, you will definitely see the benefit of forecasting your budget.

Again, the odds of my getting the forecasting one hundred percent right is very low. But honestly, the more and more I re-evaluate my budget on a weekly basis; the higher my odds are of accurately forecasting. When life happens out of my control, I adjust my forecasting tabs just like I adjust my budget. This allows me to see a bigger picture. This picture allows me to have some additional insight on the future of my finances.

Does it suck to see I could have X amount of money before Y age, and then life happens and I end up with A instead? Yes, it does sometimes, but if I did not take time to forecast and re-evaluate I would not even know X could be an X. I would probably end up with a minus-X instead; because I would not take the time to make my finances important enough to plan them out or see my potential financially.

Yes, budgeting, forecasting, and re-evaluating them all seems like more work on your end; but this work is showing you care about your financial situation and you want the best for your life. You are already taking the time to read this book, so you already have shown some dedication to changing your life. The more time you dedicate to your finances upfront the easier it will become in the long run.

At the beginning of the month, it takes about thirty minutes, for me to pay the bills and get the budget aligned along with some re-evaluating if need be. After the first week, it takes about twenty to twenty-five minutes. The third week, if nothing major happens, it takes me less than ten minutes to pay bills and to mark them paid on the budget. The remaining weeks take even less time. So during the last week in the month, I am able to dedicate time to forecasting the next month, and getting it prepared on the budget. This allows me to free up time for the following month's budget evaluations.

As you will notice, the time gets shorter and shorter for managing the monthly budget. It becomes a natural waterfall, but it is under control. If you asked the average person, without a budget, what bills are due next week, they would not be able to tell you. That is the problem with not budgeting or not re-evaluating your budget on a consistent schedule. You have no clue where your money is going, so when the month ends it is not a shocker that you are behind.

Remember the goal of this book is to gain control of your finances and to break the paycheck-to-paycheck cycle. To gain control of your finances, you have to do a little legwork to truly understand when your money is leaving your accounts. Once you put the time in, the rest will be easy and you will start to be able to manage your spending along with your budget.

Chapter 2 - Eliminating the Overhead

In the last chapter, we talked about changing our spending habits by gaining knowledge on why we spend money the way we do. Also, we talked about understanding true needs, desired wants, and other wants. In this chapter, we want to focus on how to eliminate some of the overhead placed on us financially.

The crazy part about overhead is that it may have started off as a want, but now we are financially liable to continue to pay for the want so it now becomes a need. Remember needs are things we have to pay for, or else we would suffer financially for not paying them. Most wants are turned into needs when they are purchased on credit instead of cash. Debt due to credit is truly a need that must be addressed in your budget. Unfortunately, you probably cannot afford to pay the full credit balance, and it still hurts you financially even when paying the minimum due, because of interest rates.

Debt due to credit is one of the main reasons people are living paycheck-to-paycheck. From the mortgage to the car payments to credit cards, we are constantly trying to dig ourselves out of a debt hole. Oh yeah, let us not forget about life happening. Soon as you feel you have a grip or a plan of action to alleviate debt, life happens. Now, you end up adding more debt to the debt pile. It is a constant cycle that I know most Americans are victims of.

For the remainder of this chapter, we are going to focus on some major ways to rethink the debt problems we have. This is going to suck, but honestly a lot of the time we are in debt because of ourselves. Remember the wants we purchase are truly choices we have control over. So a lot of the time, the debt that we accumulate is due to constant choices where we did not practice sound financial decision-making.

In *Set for Life*, Trench writes about how to alleviate debt by slashing the big budget items in our budget (Trench, 2017). He mentions how the little wants that we constantly battle with trying not to buy, do not really alleviate substantial space in our budget to really build cash flow. If you are someone with $10,000 in credit card debt, stopping your occasional weekly lunch with coworkers is not going to really put a dent in that $10,000 debt. The interest rates alone on the debt would barely be covered by the $10 you avoided, and you would lose the companionship with your coworkers by blowing them off every week. Now, changing how much you pay for your rent or mortgage could make a drastic change in your budget.

Again to truly be successful at your financial goals, it will take a lot of sacrifice. This chapter is going to challenge you mentally in different views of sacrifice to really open up funds in your budget. It is also going to challenge you to look at how you use credit cards, and think financially with big budget item purchases. So let us jump right in.

Living Space

Since we started talking about making a drastic change in your budget, it is only right to discuss alleviating cash flow by adjusting our living space. Now, I already know you are probably thinking, there is no amount of debt that will make me want to give up my comfortable living to move back in with my parents, or how about even better, your in-laws! I totally understand and I probably would not want to make that big of a sacrifice either; but truly to help you understand, that is the kind of sacrifice you have to be willing to make if you are truly serious about alleviating debt.

So we already know, moving in with our parents is totally on the right end of the sacrifice spectrum. Let us now move back to the left side and build our way up. In *Set for Life*, the big items in our budget can really be the easiest to change or manipulate to allow us to free up the most accessible money we currently do not have available in our budgets (Trench, 2017).

On the more relaxed side of sacrifice, renting a room in your house or apartment can be an easy move to cut your living space budget by a quarter or even half. If you have the available space in your house or apartment why not? The rooms are probably under utilized anyway. The profit from renting can now be used to save more or pay off that $10,000 credit card debt that we mentioned earlier.

If you are not familiar with AirBnB, you definitely will want to familiarize yourself especially if you plan to use the renting out a room approach. Depending on the city and proximately to attractions or business areas, you could almost quadruple the amount you receive from renting a room. AirBnB is the new hotel, and you would be surprised at the profits you can make.

Another way of alleviating some living space debt is by moving in with a roommate. It is very similar to renting out a room scenario. You automatically slash your living space budget in half or by the agreed upon split. You also cut your living space utility bills in half as well.

My first living space after college was with a roommate. I honestly thought about moving back home, but my mom was trying to charge me the same amount I would eventually pay to stay with a roommate. That was an easy decision. We would end up splitting all the bills in half, and even splurged by paying for all the movie channels, which was a bad decision at the time. The adjustment to adulthood was easier with only paying half the bills instead of paying full apartment rent plus monthly utilities. In that year, I was able to save money for a down payment to buy a new house, to go on vacation with family, and to finance a new car. Another bad decision I will address later in this book.

    A lot of my friends to whom I have given financial advice are quick to say it is hard to find compatible roommates. My rebuttal is what is worse, a horrible roommate for a year or two or living paycheck-to-paycheck with credit over your head for multiple years? These are questions you have to ask yourself, and truly understand if you are willing to make the necessary sacrifices to help yourself financially. I have heard it all. I need my own space;I do not want to let my parents hold it over my head; this mindset will not help you open up cash flow to pay off debt. No offense to you, but if you have this mindset it will potentially take you longer to break the paycheck-to-paycheck cycle.

    Shifting the focus from our current living spaces, now let us look at why we are underwater in the living space budget we have today. We often make our worst financial decision due to our "wants". I want to live in the best school district. I want to live close to nightlife. I want to live close to restaurants and shopping. Constantly, I want this and I want that, but how often when choosing a living space, do you think about how much you could save, or how much you could reduce your debt?

Too often, people move to the richest part of town just for social status, but do not actually think about how much of a burden on their budget comes with that social status. Yes, you might take rent and utilities into factor; but do you think about what else comes along with living in the wealthiest part of town? You will eventually want the same luxury car others are driving. You will eventually want the designer clothes others are wearing. If you purchase a house, you will have to keep up with maintenance on not only the house, but also the lawn so your house does not stick out from the neighbors. All of these are things just to "fit in", while your debt is constantly growing and growing.

You might not be that drastic when it comes to purchasing your living space, but, if you are honest, you did have some thoughts that did not necessarily put your financial situation in the forefront? In *Set for Life*, Trench suggests moving to the least financially affordable living space that is most comfortable to your needs in the space along with your willingness to become wealthy (Trench, 2017). I agree with him 100%. The closer you are to work, the less stress you will be daily. You will also save money on gas and wear and tear on your vehicle, but the most important thing is being financially sound when making the decision of choosing a living space. Remember your long-term goals in the decision-making, and how the negatives of the living space are just temporary for the bigger picture.

If you are already in a house where you feel the mortgage is more than you want to carry financially at the current time, you can make the decision to downsize. Why not sell the house and purchase a smaller home to help alleviate other debt? The only negative things are how others perceive the move, but remember they are not with you paying that bill every month. They definitely are not with you when you see that credit card debt rise monthly, because you cannot substantially knock the principle down. To truly beat this paycheck-to-paycheck cycle, you will have to put up blinders and not care about others' perception of your decisions. Your decisions are truly for you and your family, and to put yourself in the best situation financially.

Later in the book, we will talk about how buying a house can help you towards building wealth. But, before we can use our living space to build true wealth, we need to clear up the debt that is constantly growing in our current financial life. This is the same with all wealth building. Again, we will talk about wealth building later in the book, but you cannot build long-term wealth living paycheck-to-paycheck. I cannot state this enough, it takes true sacrifice to break the paycheck-to-paycheck cycle and to build wealth. Understanding how to sacrifice your current living space to help pay off that debt will make it ten times easier to use your living space to build long term wealth.

Cars

Earlier we talked about how transportation funds were a need. Again, transportation money is money invested to help you make more money. Whenever transportation money costs more than the money you earned, you need to reevaluate your job or income stream. In that scenario, transportation money ends up being a want. This is one major reason why car payments and leases are wants.

The money spent paying a car payment or lease is wasted money. I know you are already thinking how can I get to my job if I do not have a car? Thinking back to Trench's living space approach, if you live in close proximity to your job you can easily find alternative solutions to your transportation to and from work. Walking, biking, and taking public transportation are viable alternative solutions. Also if you are outside of a public transportation line and too far to walk, Uber and Lyft are another set of viable alternative solutions.

Some of these solutions can be extremely expensive if you are not in close proximity to your place of work. That is why it is important to eliminate the burden of long transportation to and from work by finding a reasonable living space close to your job or close to transportation to your job. The closer you are to work, the less stress you will have overall. These alternative solutions have to be financially reasonable as well. The main purpose for these solutions is to avoid a car payment at all costs. So, if transportation is costing you what you would typically pay for a car payment, you need to reevaluate your proximity to your job, and your method of transportation.

We totally want to free up money, so you can either continue to pay off debt, or have enough money to pay for a car with cash. Now, I know you are thinking, it will take me YEARS to save $30,000-$40,000 to buy my car. If you are thinking that, which most people will, you are thinking too BIG. What is the main purpose of your car? It is to get from point A to point B. Any other reason to have a special vehicle, other than to make additional income, puts purchasing that vehicle in the "wants" category.

It is time for one of my first confessions. I too used to think the same way. I read Hill Harper's "A letter to a young brother" in college. He mentioned in the book the same thing I said in the last paragraph. Your car is only a need to get you to point A to point B. If you cannot pay cash for the car, you cannot afford that car. I literally let that go in one ear and out the other. I was looking at cars I could buy before I even had a job in college. My first car mistake was purchasing a new Kia Sportage right after my junior year in college. I cannot take full credit for this one; my mom basically forced me to buy the SUV. I cannot totally blame her, because she did not have the financial knowledge to think otherwise. I was already driving her older, paid off Toyota Corolla. In her mind, a newer car meant a safer car. I was going away to Richmond for a summer internship, and she felt it was best to be in a newer car. No offense to my mother, but buying that Sportage was a bad financial decision.

The smartest thing I actually did that summer was to pay off the car payments for a year with some of the internship money. That way, I was not stressing financially while I was back in school trying to figure out how to pay the car payments and graduate at the same time. But let us take a second and think, what if I actually kept the Corolla and invested all the money I spent on car payments in the stock market. This was exactly a year or two after the market crashed. Let me make it more concrete, Amazon's stock was about the same price as my car payment in 2012. Instead of getting a new car and making fifteen payments, I could have bought fifteen shares of Amazon Stock. Today as I am writing this, Amazon's stock has grown well over 700% since 2012. With some quick math, my fifteen shares would have grown well over $20,000, and my initial investment would have only been fifteen car payments.

I am just going to jump into my second car mistake. Now, with the second one, I take full credit from my mistake and I mean full credit. I have to because I went into the car dealership by myself at 22 years old. That was the first mistake. I was fresh meat to that car salesman. Long story short, I walked away with a brand new Kia Sorento. I never took into consideration what the interest rate would be or the length of the loan. Only thing I knew was that the car payments was within my monthly budget. One of the worst financial decisions I have ever made in my life.

After talking to a few folks and realizing the mistake, I did the necessary research to knock my loan interest rate in half within a few months by refinancing my new Jeep. Another gem about financial mistakes, you should never let your mistakes linger or turn into a ripple effect of bad mistake after bad mistake. After buying the Kia Sorento, you would think I would have learned my lesson and finally listened to Hill Harper. I did not. A couple years of working full time, getting married (which meant dual income) and paying off debt, I felt I was in the position to get my "dream" car. I put a presentation together for my wife explaining how we could afford a brand new Audi A4. Again, yes, in the monthly budget I could still save and make the payments, but it was truly a financially poor decision. I thought I was making smart moves because my interest rate was 0.9%. It was still a bad financial decision. To make the decision worse, I eventually had to sell the car to get an SUV, because my "life happens" baby's car seat could not fit in the Audi. I should have just purchased the A5 coupe from the beginning.

In my personal story, you can see how even though you could be making some good, small financial decisions, making the big terrible decisions still hurts you more in the long term. The road to wealth and the non paycheck-to-paycheck life is not over night, but instead is built over time. The sole purpose of not taking on car payments is due to the additional pressure it adds on your budget. You are trying to escape the paycheck-to-paycheck cycle, and adding a car payment to that cycle is adding years to the imprisonment.

The length of the loan is not the only reason you should not finance a vehicle. Vehicles depreciate over time. So financing the car is not really the best decision, because you are losing more than just the interest of the loan every month. You are also losing the value of your car every month as well. So many people, stuck in the paycheck-to-paycheck cycle, could literally sell their cars and still have to make additional payments to cover the loan. Does that sound like a financially sound situation?

Instead of taking on car payments, try to tough it out a few years by buying an affordable car with cash. This will allow you to save additional money to help with random maintenance and to attack debt. Once you continue to practice great financially sound decisions, you will eventually be out of the cycle with the ability to save towards your "dream" car if that is your desired want.

Credit Cards

One of the primary culprits for people who find themselves underwater financially is credit card debt. I know people who have thousands of dollars in credit card debt. To be honest, for people who are not constantly making financially sound decisions, it is very easy to accrue $10,000 in credit card debt. For some people, that is one extremely bad trip to the mall. For others, it is a couple of years of life forcing them to find ways to pay this bill this month and that bill next month.

Credit companies constantly send promotions in the mail for every credit card they have in their arsenal. Credit balance transfers, no interest for the first year, and, my personal favorite, 30,000 bonus points for signing up are all examples of marketing to trigger us to sign up for another card. It is bad enough that I get asked to sign up for a clothing store credit card every time that I go to purchase clothes for an additional 20% off. Credit card temptation is EVERYWHERE; there is no surprise that over half of Americans are carrying credit card debt. I mean seriously, the mail that comes to my home is 30% bills, 10% coupons, and 60% credit card promotions.

 How beneficial would it have been to have a credit education class in high school? So many people fall victim to credit card debt, because they lack the knowledge to manage a credit card along with the inability to constantly practice financially sound decisions. Education on credit scores and credit cards in high school would reduce debt drastically.

 Let us remember how the system works; they want us to spend! Remember earlier when I talked about marketing schemes to entice us to spend our money, while on the contrary, credit cards allow us to spend money we do not have. It is not beneficial to the economy to slow down spending, instead it is beneficial to provide every individual with the surplus of credit to allow the money to never stop flowing. In America, we live in a capitalistic society and enticing folks to spend, spend, spend is apart of the money game.

I know you are thinking, thanks I wish you had provided me this information before I racked up this credit card debt. Let me start off by saying sorry if I offended you, but these are things we have to constantly reiterate to ourselves. Good financial decisions do not just happen by chance, but from constant discipline and education. Now that my apology is out of the way, stop using all credit cards if you do not have the cash to pay them off monthly!

This section is about eliminating the debt overhead. If you continue to use credit cards during your journey to escape the paycheck-to-paycheck cycle, you will never reach it. Instead, you will add additional overhead to an already bad situation. If you are serious about escaping the cycle, one of the first things you have to do is put up all your credit cards. DO NOT cancel them, for this will hurt your credit score. Instead, cut up the ones you do not plan to use again, and hide the remaining ones that you will leverage after reaching your goals.

We will talk about how to handle paying off debt later in the book, but initially you have to stop relying on credit to eliminate the overhead. Again, we cannot state this enough, credit cards will not help you escape the paycheck-to-paycheck cycle. Even after reaching your goals and becoming financially stable, credit cards will not help you stay stable unless you use them to your advantage.

I personally can say the most I have been in credit card debt was $800. It was one of the worst feelings I ever had. I recently graduated with my undergraduate degree and was coming back from a senior cruise where most of the $800 was spent. Luckily, I was starting a good job in Information Technology, and was able to pay it off with my first check. Even with that in mind, for those few weeks, it felt like a constant rain cloud over my head. For those with credit debt and are serious about a better financial life, hold on to that feeling because once you get out of the cycle you never want that feeling to come back.

Credit cards should only be used for your benefit, and not as an extension of your bank account. Remember credit is just money you do not have access to physically. So by using your credit card as an extension of your bank account, you are actually putting yourself in debt by spending money you do not have yet. Instead, you should use your credit card as a safety net or for pure benefits of the card itself.

Using the credit card as a safety net is basically using it to help protect your actual "physical" money in your bank account. I use my credit card to purchase items in my personal spending budget. I do this because in the event my card number is stolen and used for unauthorized purchases; my actual money was not stolen. Unlike your credit cards, if your debit card number and information was stolen, your actual money will be withdrawn from your accounts. On top of money being stolen, the credit card companies tend to be quicker to restore the amount to your balance and investigate the fraud after the fact. This is because it is credited money being stolen, and not actual money. The same cannot be said for your financial institution.

    I learned this the hard way in college. I bought a friend flowers online, and was accidentally enrolled into a monthly subscription. It took my bank weeks to resolve the issue, and I was only partially refunded the money that had been charged. If I used my credit card instead, I would have been credited the total amount of unauthorized purchases immediately, while the credit card company investigated the online flower company.

    The safety net is using your credit card as the middleman, but very important to remember that you are only spending money you have in the bank. With that in mind, you should pay off your credit card every month. This will allow you to never carry over a balance resulting in added interest. With this philosophy, you can use your credit card to make all your monthly purchases including bills that you are allowed to pay with credit.

With paying your bills and monthly purchases on your credit card, you can then take advantage of the benefits that come along with the card. Again, we are not getting the credit card for the purpose of financial extension of the bank account. We are picking credit cards based on the benefits the card actually offers you.

As an avid traveler, it only makes sense to pick a credit card that offers me the best travel benefits for my needs. I did not pick my credit card because of the balance it was providing me, because I knew I would only spend what my budget would allow. I instead use my credit card for free benefits. I picked my card exclusively on what I could get out of it. This is how you win the credit card game. You spend ONLY what you have budgeted, and you still reap the benefits of cash back, travel perks, and so on. Again, the key is to only spending what you have budgeted.

For those who are working on budgeting and eliminating current debt, I would highly recommend eliminating credit card use until you have paid off all debt. Even after paying off debt, you have to be mentally strong to only spend what you can pay off monthly. You have to build up the confidence of constantly making financially sound decisions before incorporating your credit card use back into your daily life. Eliminating credit card usage will allow you to focus on your current goals with only the actual money you have earned. You then can attack your goals, and once you reach them add credit card usage back solely for an additional payment safety net and for credit card benefits.

Chapter 3 - Building Savings and Eliminating Debt

In the previous chapters, we talked about changing our financial spending habits and ways of eliminating some of the overhead. With the ability to control the way we spend and adding additional income by eliminating some of the overhead, you can now focus on eliminating the debt that is holding you captive to the paycheck-to-paycheck cycle.

Too many people focus on trying to add additional income to help save money or pay off debt. So often, you find individuals who sign up for an additional job just to buy Christmas gifts, go on vacation, or save for a particular event. This second job often adds more stress to the person's life. I could write a whole book about how health is wealth, and how adding stress to your life is not helping your overall well-being.

Instead of focusing on a second job to help build savings and eliminate your existing debt, go back through the last chapter. Take the time to go through your budget, and really evaluate if your living space is too costly or if you really need that car payment. Look at your budget and see if you could slash the cable, Internet, or food budget for a while to reach your financial goals.

1st *Savings Account*

Once you are ready mentally and have the additional funds available, you are ready to open your first savings account. This initial account will help start to build some flexibility in your overall budget. This account will be used for those life emergencies you cannot forecast in your budget. This account is for car maintenance, medical emergencies, or unforeseen bills.

The amount needed in this account can vary from person to person. Remember you want to escape the paycheck-to-paycheck cycle to alleviate stress in your life. So with that in mind, the initial savings account should be enough money to help lower your stress levels while you attack your debt. In *Total Money Makeover*, Ramsey suggests that you only save $1,000 before attacking your debt (Ramsey, 2007). I believe more in the balanced approach, and that the amount saved is totally up to the person's comfort levels.

I personally am more on the conservative side and while attacking debt always had $5,000 minimum in my savings account. I remembered the feeling of carrying around the credit card debt for a couple of weeks, and did not want to feel that way ever again. With that amount, I could apply all my extra funds at debt and not have to worry at all about life events.

Can life events cost more that $5,000? Yes, but that is totally out of your control. The positive thing is if a life event happened at that time for $7,000, I would not have to look for $7,000. I would instead only need $2,000 to cover that life event. Remember, this first savings account is not for bragging about how much money you have. This account is truly for your peace of mind so you can attack your debt with some leverage.

To help come up with the "right" number, you should think about your lifestyle and what kind of unexpected financial responsibilities can come with that lifestyle. There are a lot of things to factor, but please do not overthink the value. We already know the minimum baseline should be $1,000. If you are coming from a true paycheck-to-paycheck lifestyle, that is already more than enough to ease your financial stress levels. If instead you are like me and need a little more financial peace, you can factor in some of the things you forecast as being future expenses and decide on a healthy number for yourself. I would say $5,000 is the maximum amount to have in your first savings account. So with that range, you need to decide on your perfect number to have in savings before you start to try eliminating your debt.

If you already have a savings in place, you are ahead of the pack. You already have the financial discipline or you have more income than your spending habits account for. If the latter is the case, you should really look into eliminating some additional overhead. With the additional funds, you can build your first emergency savings account then attack your debt.

Paying off Debt

If you have read other personal finance books, you would see various viewpoints on how to attack debt. I want to start of by saying every viewpoint has its place in someone's life, but again similar to the first savings account, it can vary from person to person.

One of the most popular methods is the "avalanche method" of paying off debt. You would first list all your debts from largest to smallest based on the interest rate of the debt. Keep in mind not include your mortgage as part of that list. Once you have listed them, make the minimum payment on all your debts. With the extra money in your budget, you would then want to allocate all of that money to the debt with the highest interest rate. Once you have paid off that debt, you would reallocate all additional money to the next highest debt based on interest rate. You would continue to reallocate or roll the money onto the next one with the highest interest rate until all debts are paid off.

For example, I have three outstanding debts that I owe. I have a $10,000 principle with a 4.5% interest rate on my car loan. I have $3,500 principle with a 2.75% interest rate for my student loans, and I have a $5,000 principle with an 8% interest for a personal loan I needed to help me pay bills while in college. Using the avalanche method, we would focus on the personal loan first because it has the highest interest rate at 8%. We would continue to pay the minimum payment on the two other loans, but allocate all of the extra money to the personal loan payment until it was paid off. Once eliminated, we would reallocate the money to the $10,000 car loan principal at the 4.5% interest rate. Once the car loan was paid off, we would then attack the $3,500 principle for the student loans.

Another popular method of paying off debt is the "snowball method". It is very similar to the avalanche method but has a slight twist. You would start off just like the avalanche method, but, instead of listing your debts in order from the largest to smallest by interest rate, you want to list them in order from the smallest to largest based on principal owed. Similar to the avalanche method, you would continue to pay the minimum on all your debt. Unlike the avalanche method, you want to allocate all of the additional money to the smallest debt based on its principal or money owed.

For example, I have a $2,000 principle with a 1.9% interest rate for a furniture loan. I have a $6,500 principle with a 4.5% interest rate for my car loan, and an additional $9,000 principle with an 8% interest rate for student loans. Using the snowball method, I would focus on the furniture loan first since the principle is the lowest. After paying it off, I would then focus on the next lowest principal, which is the car loan. After paying off the car loan, my additional money would be used to pay off the $9,000 principle from the student loans.

Both are solid methods of paying off debt, and both have proven to work successfully when the individual paying off debt is disciplined and willing to sacrifice for their financial goals. Remember, we have to first have the practice of sound financial decision making to truly reach our financial goals. With a lack of self-discipline, no method will work for you to pay off debt.

From a numbers standpoint, it makes total sense that the avalanche method is the best. You would attack the debt with the highest interest rate, so in the end you would eventually save more money in the long run. I personally used the avalanche method to pay off my debt. At the time, I was disciplined with my money, and did not require a push to continue to pay off debt instead of buying clothes, shoes, and other material items. I knew I would end up saving more over time, so it was the best method for me.

In *Total Money Makeover*, Ramsey highly suggests using the snowfall method (Ramsey, 2007). This method is definitely beneficial for those who continue to struggle with being disciplined in their financial spending. The snowfall method will help trick your mind into continuing to grind towards your financial goals. By paying off your lowest principal balance first, you should end up paying off a debt faster than just choosing the one with the highest interest rate. Paying off any debt will help motivate you to continue towards your financial goals. With that in mind, the snowfall method is designed to help motivate you to continue toward your financial goals.

If you already know yourself as not being disciplined financially, the snowball method is probably the best choice for you. As you pay off individual principles faster, you will continue to get that satisfaction of accomplishing your financial goals. This will help align you with continuing to knock out each goal one at a time. On the other end of the spectrum, if you are sound financially with your decision-making, I highly recommend using the avalanche method. Attacking the highest interest rate will save you more money over time. If it were based on pure numbers, the avalanche method would clearly win.

Unfortunately, eliminating debt is not purely a numbers game. It also involves the human who earns and spends the money. So before deciding on which method you want to take, I highly suggest you do a personal evaluation. You have to determine how disciplined you are towards reaching your goals, and if you will need a boost from time to time to help you stay aligned to reaching your goals.

There is nothing wrong with mixing the two from time to time. You can start off using the avalanche method, and realize it would take you a long time to pay off that particular debt. So instead of stressing and quitting your goals, you switch to snowball to gain some motivation and to check off a box on your financial goals list. You could also start off with snowball to help yourself adjust to eliminating debt. After checking off a few of your financial goals, you may realize that your financial decisions have become disciplined to align with your financial goals. You can now switch to the avalanche method to help save more money over time.

There is no 100% right or wrong way of eliminating debt with these two methods. The main question is what type of individual are you, and what is needed to keep you on the right path towards your financial goals. Keep in mind that any method of eliminating debt is better than no method. Any method of eliminating debt is better than spending the money as a consumer.

Emergency Savings Accounts

When you get to the stage of no debt, except for your mortgage, you should take some time to celebrate. Seriously, you have really accomplished the major step of escaping the paycheck-to-paycheck cycle. The majority of American citizens would trade places with you in a heartbeat. So you should take time to enjoy the accomplishment. You should go to dinner at the restaurant you never wanted to pay for or whatever is financially feasible for you to really celebrate your financial success.

Once you have celebrated, it is now time to secure your lifestyle of escaping the paycheck-to-paycheck cycle. The next step in accomplishing your next goal of stability is to start a second savings account that we call the emergency savings account. In *Total Money Makeover*, Ramsey suggests only one savings account. He suggests growing the initial $1,000 saved to equal three to six months of income (Ramsey, 2007). He totally leaves it up to you to determine that number. After reading the book, I personally was confused on how to calculate the "right" number to have in savings.

Unlike Ramsey, I really believe in having two savings accounts. The initial account you saved your $1,000-$5,000. This account should be through the same bank as your checking account. This bank should be accessible locally and in most major cities. If your financial institution does not allow for overdraft protection, you should find a new bank. First, you want your savings account to be an overdraft account for your checking account. Secondly, you want to be able to access your savings account via an ATM.

The ability to have access to this money fast is important. Remember this is your initial savings account. You need fast access to this money for emergencies. Again, one of the main causes of people falling into the paycheck-to-paycheck cycle is debt. This debt can be credit debt or personal debt. Borrowing money from family and friends is personal debt. Having access to your money will help eliminate the need to go into personal debt.

Another reason people struggle financially is unnecessary fee payments. Overdraft fees are a great way for the bank to make easy money. Setting up an overdraft account allows you to avoid these fees. Another unnecessary fee is an ATM fee, and having access to your bank locally and in major cities avoids these fees. Unnecessary fees help drive people into the paycheck-to-paycheck cycle, and they definitely are a dark cloud for some already in the cycle.

If you have not set up that initial account as mentioned above, now is definitely the time to handle that. Once everything is set up for that initial savings account and debt is paid off, you are now ready to set up the second savings account. This account should be set up with a financial institution that offers high-yield savings accounts. High-yield savings accounts offer higher interest rates than most local financial institutions.

Remember your main checking and savings account should be accessible. If you can find a bank that is accessible and offers high yield savings accounts, you would only need one savings account. If you are like me, you may have a need for having a local bank where you can actually go inside. With this need, I have my checking and initial savings account at one of America's major financial institutions. These "big banks" normally offer a below 1% interest rate on savings accounts.

Now, let us play with the numbers. I have $2,500 in my initial savings account, and I managed to save an additional $7,500 after paying off my debt. I would then have a total of $10,000 in savings. In this scenario, I have all my savings in one account at my "big bank" with an interest rate of 0.9%.

After one year, my savings account would have earned $90. Now in the second scenario, I have $2,500 in my initial savings account at my "big bank" earning 0.9% and I have $7,500 in my high yield savings account earning 2.1%. After one year, my initial savings accounts would have earned $22.50 and my high yield savings account would have earned $157.50. In my second scenario, I would have earned a total of $180.

Do you see the benefit of having a high yield savings account? Compound interest money earned is FREE money. Free money will definitely help avoid falling back into a paycheck-to-paycheck cycle. Looking at the numbers, the $7,500 in the high yield savings account earned $67.50 more dollars a year than $10,000 in my basic savings account.

With many online banks offering high yield savings accounts, it literally takes minutes to apply for one and you can do it from home or wherever you have access to Internet. This miniscule time investment will definitely pay off in the long run, and even help to keep you from falling back into the paycheck-to-paycheck cycle.

Now that you can see the benefit of having the high yield savings account, we now need to determine how much money you should actually save in this account. The first thing you want to do is to evaluate your lifestyle and living situation.

Are you in a two-income home? Do you support the family yourself off of one income? How fast can you find a job if you were fired from your job? Does your job fire or lay people off? The answers to the following questions will help determine the amount of money needed to cover significant financial emergencies.

First thing first, you want to look at your budget and highlight all your major bills. This should be easy for you if you already know what your needs are. Again, needs should be money used for necessities like your living space costs, transportation to work, food budget, and any major bills that do not fall in the desired wants or wants category. Once you have all of your needs highlighted, add all the costs up associated with your needs. I call this sum of costs, cost of living. The cost of living amount has to get paid off monthly in order for you to live comfortably and continue to provide for your family.

Once you have the cost of living amount, you want to multiply that by three. Three months of cost of living is the minimum you should save in your second savings account. Even if you have a dual income household, you want three months of cost of living in your savings account to feel secure and ensure that you could surf the toughest of financial waves in your life.

Similar to Ramsey, you will often see that having three to six months of income is the "ideal" number to save. I disagree with saving total income over saving your cost of living amount. Cost of living amount will force you to cut off the desired wants and wants in your life during a tough financial wave. So often, you see people struggling financially and try to maintain the same lifestyle. This is a direct path back into the paycheck-to-paycheck cycle. In the case of losing your job or just leaving your current job to explore new opportunities, cutting off your desired wants and wants will help motivate you to work hard to get to that lifestyle back.

On the contrary, if you already have that money in the bank to cover all your monthly expenses, you will be too relaxed in your normal lifestyle to understand the downfall you are experiencing. Do not get me wrong; I am not saying it is a bad thing to have too much money in savings. But I am saying, do not put that mental pressure on yourself. At a minimum, you should have three months of cost of living in your savings account to avoid the need for debt while looking for a new job if you were fired or laid off.

Once you have a minimum of three months of cost of living in your account, you have to determine if that amount is enough before moving on to the next financial step. This goes back to asking yourself if you are in a dual income household or how fast can you get a job in the event of losing your current one. If you are in a dual income household, the three months could be enough. If the lowest income of the two can cover the cost of living amount monthly, three months is definitely enough to feel comfortable in case one of the two incomes disappears. If the lower of the two cannot cover the cost of living amount monthly, saving an additional month or two will help with that deficiency.

Now, let us evaluate if you had a single household income. Is three months of the cost of living amount monthly enough to feel secure in the event you lose your job? To answer this question, we need to know how strong the market is for your occupation. If you work in Information Technology and lose your job, you might be able to find a job within a couple weeks to a month. If you work in a field that takes longer to find a job, you have to factor that in as well.

Above that, you have to factor in if your job typically fires people or lays them off. When you are laid off, you have the ability to claim unemployment to help offset the missing income until you find a new job. The last variable is if your job is known for giving severance packages. If so, you can factor the severance package calculation in with the unemployment income. I personally would not rely on the severance package calculation in figuring how much to save. It is not consistent enough for you to really forecast.

With those variables laid out, I am pretty sure your mind is racing, coming up with other factors that could help calculate how much you should have in that second savings account. Let me help you with the stress by saying; do not take long to evaluate it. The maximum you should have is six months of the cost of living amount. Six months should be a substantial amount to help you survive the biggest of financial waves. Of course, you cannot just sit around on a six-month vacation. At a minimum, you should be searching for a job. If you are truly struggling to find a job in your previous field, you can always find a more available job to help offset the expenses going out of the account during this time. This job might not be the income you are used to making, but it will help circumvent your path back to the paycheck-to-paycheck cycle.

Keep in mind; the emergency savings accounts are truly self-defined. They are for emergencies! They should not be used for confidence boosters or brag to your friends on social media about your accomplishments. They are your safe haven from the paycheck-to-paycheck cycle. If you ever have to dip into them, your first goal should be to replace the amount as soon as possible. As I tell my friends often, would you rather borrow money from yourself or someone else?

Chapter 4 - Saving for Wealth

Once you have come to the point of saving three to six months of cost of living expenses, you have basically escaped the paycheck-to-paycheck cycle. Your stress levels should be down, and honestly you should wake up with a big smile on your face everyday. You have accomplished what so many people dream about accomplishing. Please, sit down and take a moment to celebrate your win.

Again, use this time to celebrate your accomplishments and do something you would not normally do. If it is a vacation, save the money towards it and go! If it is a fancy dinner, you should get dressed up and enjoy that steak and potatoes. Better yet, take photos and post on social media to show off your accomplishment! I say these things, because now it is time for a new financial challenge. That challenge is called building WEALTH!

Yes, I said building wealth, and I did not say becoming rich. Being rich is a mentality. You can have all the money in the world, but if you spend it all, you will not be wealthy. Being rich is thinking a dollar amount will make you happy, but it will not. You can have six months of income saved and still be unhappy. You can have millions and millions of dollars and still be unhappy. Your goal should never be to become rich, but instead to become wealthy.

With the process laid out of escaping the paycheck-to-paycheck cycle, you have already laid the foundation down to become wealthy and maintaining that wealth. Again, it starts off with a financially focused mind on savings versus consuming. Second, it starts with eliminating debt. Then, it continues with the building of savings to help keep you from falling back into the cycle. Next, we will build real wealth by utilizing our foundation to help drive us into making sound financial decisions.

Buying a House

Reading the title "Buying a House" sounds like you are spending money instead of building savings and wealth. You are going to initially spend money in the forefront but reap the benefits in the end. Keep that in mind while continuing to read because all wealth building investments will require some initial investment, which will reap benefits in the long run. The first of them will be buying a home.

If you already purchased a home, I applaud you, but please do not skip this section. There will be tips that you can use to purchase a new home or rethink the way you are currently managing your current mortgage. For those who do not own a home or have a mortgage, this section is specifically for you!

Owning a home is more than just a lifestyle decision. I would honestly say that owning a home is just as much a financial decision as a lifestyle decision. If you are renting a house or apartment, when it is time to move, will you receive any of the investment you spent paying that rent? No, that is due to not having ownership of that living space.

Though there are occasions when renting short term can be beneficial financially compared to buying a home short term, the overall concept of renting is basically throwing your money away. As a renter, you are still only a consumer. You have no financial benefit after renting for 25-30 years. On the contrary, if you purchase a house with a conventional 30-year loan, you will own that home after the loan is paid off. Another benefit to owning a home is that your home's worth can potentially go up in value. Now, some critics will say that the value can go down, which is true, but even if the home has lost its value, it would not lose all of it's value in comparison to renting.

Buying a home may seem very daunting, but it really is broken down into two steps. The steps are securing financing and choosing a home. Securing financing is the most confusing issue for most people. Part of that problem is not being fully knowledgeable about all your financing options. Traditionally, you would hear people say to save 20% of your expected home value for a deposit. When actuality, a 20% deposit is not the only way to gain financing for a home.

It is highly suggested to purchase a home by putting down a 20% down payment to avoid private mortgage insurance, but it is not the only option. Would you rather pay approximately 1% of your mortgage towards private mortgage insurance, PMI, or continue to pay rent throwing away 100% of your investment? If I were you, I definitely would rather pay the insurance. I say that especially if saving 20% for a house would take years and years to accomplish.

Now, if you can save 20% in a short amount of time, it makes more sense to buy the home once you have your down payment in place. Avoiding PMI is a great step to take, but not great for those renting for a long time trying to avoid it. Instead, there are several options for securing a mortgage loan without having a full 20% to put down. I will only cover conventional loans, because all others are not good for financial stability. Conventional loans are consistent, and the mortgage payment does not drastically fluctuate over time.

The first of those options is for first time homebuyers. This conventional loan is called the FHA (Federal Housing Authority) loan. This loan is only for first time homebuyers. If you have a credit score above 580, you can qualify for this loan with only a 3.5% down payment. If you have a credit score between a 500-580, you can qualify for this loan with only a 10% down payment. The only downside is that PMI (Private Mortgage Insurance) is built into the loan. PMI is additional to the interest due, which takes away from paying the loan's principal down faster.

The FHA loan is perfect for individuals who understand that they are paying too much money for rent compared to what they would pay with a mortgage. A quick google search for "FHA loan lenders" will provide a list of the top lenders for accessing a FHA loan. Again, this loan is only for first time homebuyers. But, the loan is very beneficial to avoiding the rent trap.

Another avenue for securing a conventional loan without 20% is via a non-profit company named NACA. NACA stands for Neighborhood Assistance Corporation of America. Their sole purpose is to help individuals secure homes without being taken advantage of by financial intuitions. NACA guarantees all individuals will have the same mortgage experience of no down payment, no closing costs, no credit score consideration, and below market interest rates on their mortgages.

I am very familiar with NACA, because I purchased my first home through them. I know others who have purchased with them, and I know others who decided to go with a conventional loan directly from a financial institution. NACA can be very beneficial for individuals who have the patience to buy a home with smart financial decision-making.

One of the main downsides of NACA is the length of the process to secure the mortgage, especially for the individuals who decided to not use NACA because they found a home they really liked prior to attempting to secure financing. So instead of going through NACA, they needed a quicker time line to secure their financing, which most financial institutions can provide. I am a firm believer in securing financing first before choosing a home. This will allow you to choose the home with your financially sound hat on versus what you think you can afford hypothetically. Also from personal experience, those who are patient during the home purchasing process come out better financially and purchase a more stable home due to NACA's tough home evaluation process.

NACA is definitely good for individuals moving into a home with family and do not want to use the home for investment opportunities. If you are that individual, I cannot explain enough how beneficial NACA can be to you. NACA does not have an income limit, but instead has a maximum house cost, which varies by state. For more information on NACA, please go to naca.com and familiarize yourself with the organization. If you decided to secure your mortgage loan via NACA, the process is pretty simple. The NACA loan agent will work with you on a plan to secure the loan. They will want proof of budget stability, and may require you to hit financial goals to prove you are able to maintain a mortgage payment over time. Once those goals are met, you are then pre-approved and allowed to start searching for a property.

If you are purchasing a home as an investment, NACA is not for you. Instead, you can use a traditional conventional loan to purchase your home. Even with a conventional loan, you are not required to pay a down payment of 20%. It will vary depending on your credit score. On my second home purchase, I did not use NACA due to the cost of the home being higher than NACA's threshold. I secured a conventional loan, and I was only required to pay a down payment of 5%. The down payment can vary, but you can get that information anytime from a lender.

Now that you know your options on the types of mortgage loans, the next step is to save for your down payment. You already have a savings mindset, so this step should be easier than it would have been at the beginning of this book. You deposit the additional down payment in your second savings account until you are ready to secure your loan.

Once you have the down payment saved, the next step is to shop for your mortgage loan. Every lender will have a different set of criteria for their loans. Interest rates and closing costs will vary depending on the lender, so it is very important to shop around and compare each vendor. DO NOT and I say do not secure the mortgage loan with the first lender without shopping around first. You want to make the best financial decision when buying a home, because it will be one of the biggest financial purchases of your life. With that in mind, do not rush the process.

After securing your loan or better to say that you pre-qualify for a loan, you know the amount of a house you can ideally purchase. You can now consult with a real estate agent to help find your new home. The next step can be different for two types of individuals. You will either be a home investor or a home dweller. Either type is perfectly fine.

One main thing when purchasing a home for both types is finding a home with equity built into the home at purchase time. Equity is the difference between the amount of the loan or home listing price versus what the home is actually worth. To state it in common English, you want to find a home that is worth more than it is listed for sale.

Your real estate agent will be your guide for that. You want to tell them your pre-qualified loan amount and what you are looking for in a home. Purchasing a home with equity is already boosting your financial wealth. Instead of taking the full debt of the mortgage, you offset it with equity. You can also use that equity for additional money if you run into another life event.

For the home dweller, this is the perfect scenario. You purchased a home below market value, and you can now focus on the next steps of building wealth. For the home investor, equity is not the end of your goals. The home investor is looking for a home that will turn out to be a better investment than just the market value of the house.

In *Set for Life*, Trench writes about house hacking as being the best way to buy a home for those who want to become super wealthy via real estate (Trench, 2017). House hacking allows individuals to purchase the house and rent out rooms or sections of the home to help offset the mortgage payments or to pay them in full. House hacking is a great approach for the home investor. Not only do you benefit from the equity in the house at purchase, but also you are staying in the house with little to none of your budget going towards paying the mortgage payment.

For home investors, this is the perfect scenario to allow you to save or use equity to purchase an additional investment property. If you use the same principles of patience and finding a home with equity, you can easily have several investment homes within several years. Accumulating real estate is one of the best ways of building and securing wealth. Home investing sounds like a no brainer, but you have to have the time and mental capacity to do it. Home investing is really a second job, and requires additional investment money to help maintain the quality of the home overtime.

Before purchasing a home, you have to figure out which type of homebuyer you are. It is totally ok to start off as a home dweller and transition into the home investor. Honestly, I am on the conservative side, and I am currently a home dweller. I have equity in my home available for use to invest in additional properties, but do not want to take the risk of buying additional investment properties or renting space in my home at this current time. Eventually, I can see myself buying investment properties, but at this time I am content with my financial stability.

That is totally my perspective, but once you come up with what type of home buyer you are, it helps with finding the ideal house for your needs and wants. If you decide that you are a home dweller, the next step is pretty simple. You want to find the most affordable house that fits your needs and probably some of your wants. Again, it will be beneficial to find a house listed on the market for less than it's worth. Finding a house with equity can be very hard depending on the current market when you decide to buy, but if you can find one it will be in your best interest.

I know you are probably thinking, but what if I want x, y, and z in my house but it is not the most affordable? Then, you have to lean on the early chapter of why you want x, y, and z in the house. Remember, your living space will be one of your biggest expenses. Do you want to pay for what you need or for what you want? Do you want to buy a house to show off to people who barely come over or do you require just enough house space to make your family comfortable? These are questions you seriously have to ask yourself.

Do not make the mistake I made. When I purchased my first home through NACA, I was patient and did not rush the process. My patience lead me into a very affordable home with more than enough space than I needed, and the home had equity in it at purchase time. On the second house, I was not nearly as patient as buying the first one. I knew I really liked the neighborhood and school system. Beyond that, the process was a total rush. We randomly visited the neighborhood one day, with no intention of buying a new home anytime soon. Upon viewing the model home, we were definitely amazed and caught completely off guard. Next thing I knew, I was being pitched on how the lots were selling; and if I really wanted to be in the neighborhood, I would have to make a quick decision on how to secure a mortgage loan.

Less than a month or two later, my house was sold and we were moving into a temporary two bedroom apartment until the new house was built. Now, I cannot say the whole process was a complete disaster. The selling market was really strong, and my first house was on the market for less than a week. I made the decision to sell my house due to the equity in the home already and having lived there for about six years. Also, I was able to get into the neighborhood I wanted to live in and have an awesome second level porch that I had always dreamed about.

That being said, I could have been smarter and had more patience during the whole process. I did not shop around for my second mortgage, and just went with the builder's preferred lender. That was a no-no; please shop around for the best deal! I did not shop around for a real estate agent, but instead went with an agent who worked with several other home purchasers from the neighborhood. Most of all I did not negotiate enough. I did not negotiate with the builder for more feature money. I did not negotiate with the real estate agent on commission percentage. I did not negotiate with the buyer of my first home. All of those were pure money saving mistakes. Do not make the same mistakes I made. During the home purchasing phase, anything is negotiable and having patience will help you get the results you want.

This is a perfect transition to the home investors process of buying a home. The fact is that you should negotiate down to the penny on everything during the buying process. Every dollar matters to you because this as an investment opportunity used solely to help increase your wealth. With home investors, the most important aspect of the first home should be how to utilize the house to make money to help offset my mortgage payment. Some questions to think about are: Do I want a basement to rent out? Do I want a multi-unit house so I can live in one unit and rent the others out? Do I want a traditional home that I can rent individual rooms out until I want to sell or move out? These are major questions to think about.

Those questions are all examples of house hacking. House hacking literally catapults you into a position to keep raising your capital for the next investment. Again, if you are able to find a living space with equity, it gives you even more cash flow for investing. You are allowed to take a loan for a percentage of the equity for your benefit. Now, I am not telling you to take out a home equity loan to splurge on material items, but instead showing you how you can access cash for the next investment. The key is being very patient and finding the best home for your needs and wants. Once finding that home, you want to focus on continuing to grow your capital for the next investment. Once you are financially stable to take on the next investment, you repeat the same steps.

Please keep in mind; you have to really ask yourself if you are built to take on the risk of being a home investor over a home dweller. Again, I admit I am a home dweller and I hold no fault against myself for being so. I totally own it. You have to too. Everyone's opinions about your living space are not going to pay your bills. Most average working folks are home dwellers, and a lot of them are content with being dwellers. You have to take a real look at what you want out of your life and living space, and make the best decisions going forward. You have to be 100% content in the decision you make.

Retirement Investing

After purchasing a house, you should be clearly out of the paycheck-to-paycheck cycle and have enough money in your savings to cover emergencies. So what is the next step to take to help prevent you from falling back into the paycheck-to-paycheck cycle? Remember, you have already accomplished more than a lot of your peers. The only debt you should have right now is your mortgage, but we have a few things to focus on before we attempt to pay off the mortgage. The key to avoiding the paycheck-to-paycheck cycle lifestyle is to continuously build wealth.

We already have emergency savings in place to help pay any life events we encounter, but high-yield savings accounts only payout around 2% interest annually. After purchasing a house, the next goal is to continue to save. Instead of just saving at that 2% interest rate, we want to allocate our money in other financial vehicles that will produce higher return costs. This is called investing!

Financial investing is taking some of your hard earned money and investing it into the stock market. The catch with investing is that your investment is not guaranteed to make a positive return of money. Often investments lose some of its initial value, and sometimes it loses all of its initial value. This truth about investing scares a lot of people, and hinders them from investing. Instead, we fall back into the consumer mindset thinking I would rather spend the money on my desires and wants instead of watching it lose value. This mindset can lead you back into the paycheck-to-paycheck cycle.

Instead, I am here to help you navigate the world of building wealth, and you cannot build wealth without investing your hard earned money to make more money for you. In this section, we will cover essential ways of building your retirement. Remember, the goal is to never go back to the paycheck-to-paycheck cycle. We are not guaranteed to work for the rest of our lives, and it is important to prepare for your retirement day. The more you invest towards that day, the faster the day will arrive.

I highly recommend reading J.L. Collins's *The Simple Path to Wealth*. It is a great book on simple investing and breaks down the confusing world of investing (Collins, 2016). In this section, I will try my best to cover the various topics that Mr. Collins discusses in his book. I will also detail various retirement investments I have in place.

Traditional 401k, 403b, and 457 plans

Most people are familiar with 401k plans, but for those who are new to the investment world 401k, 403b, and 457 plans are basically investment opportunities offered by your employer. 401k plans are tax-exempt plans offered by the majority of employers to help employees save toward retirement tax-free.

Traditional 401k plans allow the employee to invest pre-tax money and allow that money to grow tax-free until withdrawn. The eligible age to withdraw money penalty free is 59 ½ as I currently write this book. Any withdrawals from the plan prior to the investor turning 59 ½ can result in a 10% early withdrawal tax penalty. Of course there are loopholes to accessing the money, but our main focus is to save for retirement so we will not cover the loopholes. We want that money to be available in retirement!

403b plans are very similar to 401k plans, but 403b plans are offered from tax-exempt and non-profit employers such as churches and schools. These plans often lack the investment opportunities that 401k's offer, but otherwise the same rules apply. Eligible withdrawal age is 59 ½ and any withdrawals before hand will result in a 10% early withdrawal tax penalty.

457 plans are similar to both of the previous plans, but do not have a 10% early withdrawal penalty. State and local government employers offer 457 plans, along with some special non-profit organizations. If the employer offers both a 401k and 457 plans, you can contribute the max of both independently.

Speaking of max contributions, at this current time, 2019, the max for contributions to all above plans is $19,000 a year for anyone under 50. Once 50 or older, you can make additional catch-up contributions up to $6000 a year for employer plans. Like all other numbers in this book, I highly suggest researching the current figures since these will fluctuate throughout the years.

The biggest benefit of these plans is that they are tax-free and lower your income for tax purposes. Another benefit of the plans is employer investment matching. Some employers will offer a match up to a certain percentage. What does that sound like? It sounds like free money to me. I highly suggest that the minimum you invest be equal to the employer matching percentage.

When I first started working after college, my employer offered a 6% percent match from day 1. I initially set my 401k-contribution percentage to 6% and never looked back. Believe me you do not want to miss out on the free money, and you will definitely not miss the money you invested if you never receive it initially. If you have not taken advantage of your employer match contribution, I HIGHLY suggest that you add it as a top priority on your to do list.

Now with that being said, most employer matches are not a high percentage. I have heard of match percentages ranging from 2-10% of your salary up to 50-100% match of the contribution. A lot of financial gurus, including Dave Ramsey, believe the minimum to invest for retirement is 15% of your total home income. I am more on the flexible side. The absolute minimum invested should be the company's match percentage. From there, you can increase the percentage as you please.

One way to increase the percentage, which I am now implementing, is increasing it whenever you receive a raise. At my current employer, it is internal knowledge that 2-3% raises are expected every year. Instead of allowing that money to hit my budget yearly, I will keep my current standard of living and apply the extra money towards my 401k investment contributions. I will continue to do so until my contributions are at 15% of my income or the max contribution limit if it is reached before the 15% contribution. This will allow me to maximize my retirement funds, lower my current income tax, and stay grounded spending wise.

If you are at the point of having your emergency savings in place, only debt is mortgage, and have extra money in your budget, I highly recommend investing 15% of your income in employer plans before spending the money on material items or even investing in the stock market via other channels.

Traditional IRA's

Now, what are your options if you are an entrepreneur or better yet, you have your 401k maxed out and want to invest additional money towards retirement? The answer is an IRA or individual retirement account. IRA's allow you to invest already taxed money, but you are allowed to deduct the investment amount from your overall earnings when tax time comes. The earnings on the invested money will grow tax-free until you make withdrawals.

Similar to the employer plans, withdrawals from IRA's before the age of 59 ½ will result in a 10% early withdrawal tax penalty. IRA's have a different maximum contribution limit. As of 2019, you are only allowed to contribute up to $6000 annually, and if you are older than 50, $7000 annually. Again, there are loopholes on withdrawals from IRA's such as first time home buyer withdraws, but I really want you to focus on not withdrawing money before the age of 59 ½. Similar to your emergency fund, retirement investments are ensuring that you will never go back to paycheck-to-paycheck cycle even at an old age.

Unlike employer plans, your IRA contributions are yours to keep until you are ready to retire. That being said, employer plans occasionally stay intact when you and the employer part ways, but often the employer will either pay out the plan in cash or allow you to roll the money into an IRA. Listen clearly, DO NOT TAKE THE MONEY IN CASH! If you are under 59 ½ you will be responsible for the 10% withdrawal tax penalty and the taxes on any gains from the money.

I have a close friend who recently parted ways with his first employer out of undergraduate school. He had over $100,000 in a 401k plan at the time. Instead of rolling the money into an IRA, he opted to take the money in cash. With the 10% withdrawal penalty, he was automatically on the hook for $10,000. He also had to pay taxes on the total amount withdrawn. He was making six figures at the time and the head of the household since his wife was a stay at home mother. If you account for the extra money from the withdrawal, he was clearly in the 35% tax bracket for that year. He was responsible to pay another $35,000 in taxes and that was only federal taxes. With quick math and not including state taxes, he only received a max of $55,000 and now has to start over as far as retirement saving.

Now on the other hand, let us say he rolled that money into an IRA. He did not make any additional payments and his investments averaged a 6% return yearly for 30 years. He would then have over $500,000 in the IRA. He literally left $445,000 on the table. So you might already be thinking, well he will have to pay taxes on the $500,000 at withdrawal. Even if he withdrew all the money at 60 at the worst current tax rates, he will still net $360,000. On the bright side of things, he used the money to pay off debt, but still he missed out on a huge chunk of money and now has to rebuild the retirement savings nest egg he once had.

Roth Options

To add more complexity to retirement investing, all of the plans above, except 537's, have Roth options on top of traditional plans. For the 401k and 403b plans, Roth options vary based on your employer, but far as an IRA you can opt for a ROTH IRA over a traditional IRA. So what is Roth and what makes it different?

Roth options basically allow you to pay the taxes upfront and withdraw the money later tax-free. The money you invest and the gains from those investments will be taxed at your current tax rate. The withdrawals will not be taxed at all when you withdraw. Similar to traditional accounts, Roth plans have a maximum contribution amount. 401k plans are limited to the $19,000 limit annually whether it is a traditional plan, Roth plan, or a combination of both. Similar to the 401k plans, IRA plans are limited to the $6000 limit annually whether it is a traditional plan, Roth plan, or a combination of both. Basically if you are leveraging both a traditional and Roth plan, your cap is the total of both plans contributions.

Unlike traditional IRA's, Roth IRA's contributions must be under an income limit. As of 2019, single individuals or heads of households can contribute up to the max if they make less than $122,000. For couples filing jointly, the maximum contribution income limit is $193,000. You may be eligible for partial payments if your income is less than $137,000 and $203,000 for single individuals or heads of households and married couples filing jointly, respectfully. The amount is based on an IRS calculation, and I suggest you research to make sure you do not go over the limit.

The main benefit of Roth plans is purely tax benefits. If you are in a low tax bracket and foresee rising to a higher one at time of retirement, it is beneficial for you to utilize Roth plans. An additional benefit is that Roth plans do not currently require RMDs or required minimum distributions. RMDs are a set amount of money you MUST withdraw from 401k and IRA plans once you turn 70. The RMD amount grows every year after 70. Many utilize Roth plans to help offset the effects of RMDs. Roth plans can be handed over to your beneficiaries tax-free and do not require you to take withdrawals at 70 or any other age.

Again, I highly recommend researching the current figures discussed in this book since it is written in 2019 and laws often change. Also, if you invested the time to read my book, please invest the time to read *The Simple Path to Wealth*. Mr. Collins covers all plans, RMDs, and a lot more investment options and examples that will help you make sound financial decisions (Collins, 2016).

HSAs

A new non-traditional retirement account is an HSA or Health Savings Account. HSAs are often confused with Health Savings Plans. Both allow you to set aside pre-tax income for medical payments. Unlike HSAs, Health Savings Plans are vacated at the end of the year so whatever you do not use you lose.

Traditional HSAs are used to cover medical costs throughout the year. One requirement of an HSA plan is that it has to be combined with a high deductible health plan for you to be able to contribute to it. The maximum contribution, as of 2019, is $3500 for single individuals and $7000 for families annually. If you are 55 or older, you are eligible to make an additional $1000 deposit annually. These limits include your contributions along with any employer contributions.

HSAs carry over from year to year, and the biggest benefit making it a non-traditional retirement account is that you can invest your HSA funds. All withdrawals before the age of 65 have to be for qualified medical payments. After the age of 65, you can withdraw from your HSA for qualified and non-qualified withdrawals. With this in mind, HSAs have become a non-traditional way of saving for retirement.

If you are very young and healthy, I recommend opting for a high deductible plan and contributing the max to your HSA. If you happen to have medical bills throughout the year, I would pay any bill under $500 out of pocket, and use HSA funds to pay any bill above $500 on a payment schedule. This will allow you to basically pay the bill off over time with HSA money while still contributing towards your HSA. You will still be able to invest the majority of the funds in your HSA as well.

I personally have a high deductible plan covering my daughter and myself; my wife receives free health care from her employer. I contribute almost to the max contribution, and plan to max it out next benefit enrollment season. I currently do not have any of the funds in investments, but plan to do so after having a second child. I am more conservative, and want to ensure my money is there for paying childbirth bills. After having that child, I will invest most of the money in the account while leaving $3000-$4000 in cash for any unexpected medical bills.

College Savings for Children

If you financially made it to this point, you are in great shape! You put the paycheck-to-paycheck cycle far behind you and are on the road and not looking back. So what is next? Again, you can look at that mortgage over your head, but I do not believe we are quite there yet to use funds to pay it off. Instead, I would focus on setting up the future for your children.

Many often opt to use the education loophole to withdraw money from an IRA or Roth IRA to help pay for their children's education. Again, I highly recommend using retirement withdrawals only for retirement. With that in mind, I suggest using a 529 plan for your children's educational needs. The sole purpose of saving for your children's education is purely for their education and nothing else. Since Roth IRA plans are for retirement savings, I recommend only withdrawing for retirement needs or to pass to heirs. Since 529 plans are for college savings, I recommend using 529 plans to help save for your children's educational needs.

One of the best benefits of 529 plans is that the beneficiary can use it for high school, undergraduate college, or graduate school costs. If that person receives a full scholarship, they can withdraw the invested money from the 529 plan tax-free up to the scholarship amount. If the beneficiary decides not to go to college, you can always change the beneficiary on the account to another child, niece, nephew, or anyone in the family.

In the worst case if you withdraw any funds from the 529 plan that are not education eligible, you will have to pay a 10% withdrawal penalty. Educational eligible purchases include books. I highly recommend looking up all of the eligible purchases before withdrawing from your children's 529 plan.

As for which 529 plan to choose, I would stay away from state plans. They limit the beneficiary to only using the plan in the state of purchase. Instead, I highly recommend opening up a 529 plan at your favorite investment firm. I personally have a plan open at Vanguard. I invested $3000 initially, and I have recurring monthly payments of $100 going into the plan. When I have a second child, I plan to do the same thing. The ultimate goal is setting up your children for a better life than the one you were given.

Forecasted Savings

Now, it is time to reflect and think about how far you have come or will come at this point. You have successfully escaped the paycheck-to-paycheck cycle, built your emergency fund, developed a habit for retirement savings, and even started saving for your children's educational needs. So again, you may be thinking so what now? Let us go back to talking about our budget, and the need for forecasting.

During your road of escaping the paycheck-to-paycheck cycle and building wealth, you will never have a linear progression. There will be times you have to use some of your savings and then build it back up before proceeding. Remember we cannot control life events and that is why we build up our emergency savings fund. On the contrary if we practice forecasting, we can plan accordingly to help us better off financially over time.

In an earlier section about budgeting, it was important to forecast so that you are not caught off guard by unexpected bills. Now, nothing has changed much except that you are no longer in the paycheck-to-paycheck cycle, and you should have a decent amount of cash in your emergency savings plan to plan for the future. At this moment, you are ready to save for future expenses. These expenses can be a new car, real estate, or a dream vacation. You have the room now to save with no drastic overhead to worry about. Yes, you have a mortgage, but you would be paying the majority or more of that money on rent if you did not purchase a house. Also, if you have additional desired wants in life, there is no rush to pay the house off immediately.

On the conservative side of the house is Dave Ramsey. Ramsey believes that the next step, after setting up 401k and children's education plans, is to throw all extra money on your mortgage (Ramsey, 2007). I do not totally agree with this method. Again, I am conservative, but I also believe that you have to enjoy life as well. Using all of your extra money to pay off your mortgage can definitely help you pay it off fast. Life after paying off your mortgage is a dream. Just thinking about the amount of stress reduced by paying off my mortgage makes me smile, but playing devil's advocate, what if I die before I make it to the dream?

My philosophy is needs first and desired wants second. To live life accordingly, you have to make reasonable financial room for your desired wants. Your desired wants should bring you just as much joy as paying off your mortgage. If paying off your mortgage is a desired want, you should attack your mortgage with all of your available capacity. If paying off your mortgage is not on the top of your desired wants list then it is just a want. Remember from the budgeting section, wants come after needs and desired wants.

Chapter 5 - Investments for Wealth

In the previous section, we discussed various options you have for savings toward retirement and ultimate wealth. Though we covered the basics of prioritizing your savings, we did not cover how to invest your savings to make more money for you. There is nothing better than making money while not actually working.

If you followed the advice in the book, you should have your emergency savings in a high-yield savings account. This account should return 2% plus interest on the money in your account. This account is your first investment. So how do we beat the interest rate from the savings account with cash invested? We invest wisely! Again, I cannot take all the credit for the information in this chapter. I highly recommend reading *The Simple Path to Wealth*. Mr. Collins goes really in-depth on the history of the stock market and investments (Collins, 2016). He was an artist at making investments simple for uneducated investors.

One major investment note is that you do not have to buy stocks directly for your savings to produce significant earnings. If you ever read anything on investing, you probably heard diversify, diversify, and diversify! That advice is totally correct, but do you really have to diversify all your assets?

Before reading *The Simple Path to Wealth*, I had a conversation with a financial adviser on the same topic. Like most financial advisors, he mentioned how you can put money here, there, and elsewhere. The conversation often becomes very confusing really fast. I honestly think it is part of their objective so the financial advisor can manage your money for you. Make investing complicated so we can capitalize on the weak. The good news is that it is not required that you have a super diversified investment portfolio to make money and sustain from losing money in the market.

It really is as simple as allocating your investments to a low cost total stock market index funds and total bond market index funds. Some people will call this bluff and say that your portfolio is not diverse enough or even better you are limiting the return on your investments. Are they right? Maybe half right, but not entirely. Are you diverse enough? In my opinion, yes you are. We will cover why in a second. Are you limiting the return on your investments? Yes, but that is by default. Most of this money is your retirement money. After living paycheck-to-paycheck, do you really want to gamble with your life earnings? I would assume no!

Too often, financial advisors over complicate investing so they can benefit from your money. Now, am I completely against financial advisors? No, some individuals have a substantial amount of wealth that would be extremely hard for them to manage their assets themselves. No hard feelings, but I am going to assume that the majority of the folks reading this book do not have a substantial amount of wealth. For those individuals who do have a substantial amount of wealth, congrats because you are in the exclusive 1% of the United States. So my suggestion to you is, do not hire a financial advisor unless you are incapable of managing your money yourself. If you are capable of earning money, you should be able to manage it as well.

We are going to keep it very simple for this is not a book on investing. Do not invest your hard earned money directly in stocks unless you are willing to lose all or most of the money invested. Mutual funds, specifically low cost total market index funds, are the way to go for the majority of your investment depending on your age. Bonds are a great way to diversify your portfolio to help minimize the lost you can take. If you are unaware, the market changes both positively and negatively and you definitely can take a lost and I mean really fast. I will definitely share my stock story later on.

Stocks

What are stocks? Stocks are shares sold by corporations to raise capital to operate their company and to hopefully raise profits. When you purchase stock, you effectively purchase equity in the company of the stock you purchased. Does that mean you own the company? Not exactly, you own equity in the company as an investor.

For instance, let us say you own 30 shares of a total 90 shares of a company. Do you own 1/3 of the company? Not entirely, you own 1/3 of the equity in the company. You do not have power over the assets or the operations of the company. Your stocks do give you voting power when it is time to vote on board of directors and various topics during the annual meeting. You cannot claim ownership of the buildings the companies own. Even more, just because you own stock does not guarantee discounts from the company. It would be amazing to receive 15% off all Apple products due to owning a couple shares of Apple stocks.

Stocks are one of the most basic investments an investor can own. Stocks can offer great returns, as well as, bad returns. This is due to stock values being very volatile. Stock values go up and down throughout the day. So why does this happen? First off, market demand drives the values. The more individuals buying a stock, the higher the stock price rises. People start to sell the stock; the stock price declines. The craziest thing about the market is that Wall Street plays a huge role in driving the volatility. Analysts make money daily by basically driving prices up and down by providing data and information from each company in the market. Information on a new product, information on a bad product, organization issues, and many other factors influence the valuation of a company and the buying and selling flow of the stock market.

The issue with buying stocks is people think that they can hand pick stocks to make them a fortune similar to Warren Buffet. Often, those individuals find out pretty fast they are not Warren Buffet. The odds of you hitting a home run when it comes to stock picking is very low. We cannot predict the future. We have to also remember that the main goal of investing is building wealth, and not so much of the short-term gains you receive. Yes, some stocks might have plus 12% returns in a day, week, or month, but then they can turn around and plummet 50% in a quarter or year.

This is a great time for my failure stock story. Like most people, I was scared of the stock market and did not fully understand how to invest. I actually had a Roth IRA with money invested in a mutual fund, but I really wanted to test the stock market out more. I downloaded Robinhood, a mobile app that allows you to trade via your phone. I transferred $100 and decided to go all in on a cannabis stock since in 2018-2019 weed stocks were popular. I kid you not; the stock value rose over 100% by market opening the next day. So like the uneducated investor I was, I realigned my Roth IRA investments from the mutual fund to of course, the cannabis stock. I thought I was about to make double my money in a Roth IRA, but I was enlightened really fast. By opening the next day, my initial $100, which rose to over $200, was back down to around $115-120 by time I sold it. As for my Roth IRA, I definitely lost about $1500 in a day!

Yes, some individuals are fortunate enough to make millions in the stock market, but honestly, buying one stock is like gambling or playing the lottery. Sometimes one's fortune is pure luck. You have to remember with stock investing that you have to be willing to lose all your money when you invest it in stocks, especially stocks that can produce high returns. It is very similar to any other concept of money: the higher the return, the higher the risk.

My suggestion is do not gamble away the majority of your hard earned money buying individual stocks. Of course if you already have your retirement savings in place and have funds available, you have the flexibility to buy individual stocks and see how they work for you. The majority of the folks this book was written for are not in a position to waste their money. For those individuals, stay away from individual stock purchasing.

Mutual Funds

The craziest thing about my stock story was that the mutual fund I had the Roth IRA money invested in was returning plus 7% in less than two years. At the time, I honestly had no clue what a mutual fund actually was. I just knew it was recommended to invest in them from a financial security standpoint since their prices were less volatile than individual stocks.

Mutual funds are basically a collection of stocks from multiple different entities. Professional money managers are in charge of managing mutual funds for the fund's company. These companies or mutual fund families include Fidelity, Vanguard, and several other financial institutions. Fidelity and Vanguard are probably two of the most popular mutual fund families. Mutual funds by definition allow diversification. The mutual fund is made up of several different company stocks and not just one company. So if one company stock values decreases, the fund may remain stable if the other companies' stock values increase.

An investor would typically pick their financial institution first, the type of investment vehicle, and then the actual investment they want to allocate it to. For example, I currently have an account with Fidelity. The investment vehicle is an IRA, and I have it invested across several mutual funds. The key is that whatever institution you pick has a set of mutual funds to offer you. It makes sense that Fidelity will only allow you to invest in Fidelity mutual funds and Vanguard will only allow you to invest in Vanguard mutual funds. This is important as your start to research various mutual funds. You will want to align your financial vehicles or plans with the company that offers investing in the mutual fund of your choice.

One specific type of mutual fund that I highly suggest is index funds. These funds basically are mapped to follow stock market indexes. The two major indexes are S&P 500 and Dow Jones. These indexes are often used to describe the market as a whole. The indexes are made up of a collection of selected stocks that help drive the holistic picture of how the market is doing.

So why do I highly suggest index funds overall? The average return of the stock market in the last 30 years is around 10% annually. That 10% includes the Great Recession of 2008 in which the market crashed around 35-36%. The Great Recession lasted about one and a half years. So let those numbers really sink in. Though in a span of 18 months the market crashed 35%, it rose 10% in 30 years. This should give you some piece of mind that for long term investing, mutual funds are the way to go to build wealth.

Index funds come in different varieties, but my suggestion would be to invest in a total market index fund. Yes, you can diversify more and maybe make higher returns. My suggestion is simpler, but yet still diversified. The S&P 500 index is made up of 500 large US companies. The index follows the market, and over the last 30 years produced a return of 10% average annually. Many folks attempt to beat that average, but the odds are against them. You are better off investing in a total market index fund that holds every single publicly traded stock in the US.

The objective is to find the right total market index funds with low costs! Purchasing investments are not free, and every time your dividend is reinvested you have to pay a price. The objective is for that price to be the lowest, so you can reap the full benefit of the gains. A suggested fund to investigate is the Vanguard fund, VTSAX. The Fidelity equivalent is FSKAX. Both are total market index funds and the identifier can change so it is key to remember that they are total market index funds. The main difference is Vanguard has a $3000 minimum buy in with a 0.04% expense ratio, and an additional fee for accounts with less than $10,000. Fidelity on the other hand has a 0.015% expense ratio. The expense ratio is the percentage of the total investment charged by the fund manager. So if you have $10,000 in both VTSAX and FSKAX, you will pay a $4 fee a year to Vanguard for VTSAX and a $1.50 fee a year to Fidelity for FSKAX. Additional benefits of mutual funds are the compound interest and dividend payout that are reinvested into the fund resulting in higher returns. Disclaimer, I am not a financial advisor, but this is viable information.

Vanguard and Fidelity are not the only institutions that offer total market index funds. This is important depending on your financial institution's investment options. I would suggest finding a total market index fund that the institution provides. If the institution does not provide one, you can see if they provide an S&P market fund or Dow Jones market fund. In the worst case, you can invest your money against a target date fund. These funds will auto allocate your investment ratio from stocks to bonds the closer time gets to the target date. These are funds for individuals who are less active in their investments and simply want to select an investment and allow the money grow.

Bond Funds

We just talked about target date funds that over time reallocate stock investments into bond investments. So what are bonds exactly? Bonds are basically a loan to a company with a promise to repay the full principal amount at loan maturity along with additional payments at specific intervals.

Bond funds are a collection of individual bonds managed by professional money managers.

Since the borrower company agrees to pay the bond back in full, bonds become less volatile than stocks. That also means that bonds do not return great returns like stocks can. Since bonds are more stable, they are great for diversification against stock market volatility. As discussed before, target date mutual funds automatically reallocate stocks to bonds over time. This is great for passive investors, as they get closer to retirement. You will want less volatility in your portfolio close and during retirement. Bonds allow that stability overall.

So what is the correct ratio of stocks to bonds? It is totally up to your discretion if you are managing it yourself. Some people believe you should do 110 minus your age. This number is the percentage allocated in bonds and the left over being the percentage allocated in stocks. On the more aggressive side, you can do 120 minus your age. Surprisingly, target date funds run a bit aggressive. There are some target dates funds with target dates less than 12 years away with 75% stock allocations. The bottom line is what is your appetite for volatility, and what ratio will help you sleep better at night. Regardless of ratio, the market will have some bad years; do you have the fortitude to wait out the bad times until the market bounces back.

Non-traditional Investing for Wealth

In this chapter, we have pretty much covered traditional investing. Get a job, save money, and let it grow over time is the traditional way of building wealth through investing. At this point, you should already be out of the paycheck-to-paycheck cycle and have traditional investing in place or at least at a minimum some retirement savings in place. Now, you are trying to decide if you should keep investing traditionally, pay off your mortgage, or use other ways to build wealth. At this stage, you honestly could not go wrong investing more or paying off your mortgage, but what are the other options?

Real-Estate

One of those options that really helps build wealth over time is real estate investing. Again, I am not an expert nor is this book a real estate investing book, so we are going to cover a few ways real estate can help generate wealth over time. If you are fortunate enough to have additional extra funds or just have a drive for real estate, you can purchase additional properties with intent to rent them out for additional income. I covered house hacking earlier, and it is a great practice for beginning real estate investing. If done correctly, real estate investing can actually become your main source of income.

In today's real estate market, you can either rent your property directly to renters, or you can leverage tools like AirBnB to rent out your property similar to a hotel. I have even heard of people receiving permission from owners to rent out their space for a percentage of the revenue gained.

I have a friend who leverages AirBnB to rent out two properties. One is essentially a house hack while the other is a second investment property he owns. The house hack is the basement of his current residence. He was fortunate enough to find a house with a basement that has a separate driveway from his main driveway. He and his wife renovated the basement themselves and now have the property on AirBnB. At first, his intent was purely to help offset some of his mortgage payment. Today, that basement generates enough cash flow to pay his mortgage plus more.

The second property was initially rented out to a single renter. Once the last lease with the renter was up, they renovated the second house completely, and again posted it on AirBnB. That house is paid off and has become a cash revenue machine. Did it require him to take on some risks? Sure, he did not follow the steps of this book as far as building wealth step by step, but he understood how real estate in general builds wealth.

So what does that mean for you? If you followed the steps in this book, you would be in better shape than my friend who leveraged loans to invest in real estate. Instead think about leveraging your cash instead of borrowed money. You would immediately be in the situation he is in with the second home. Initially, it may take a huge investment, but you, your children, and your children's children can benefit over time.

Dave Ramsey preaches only using cash for investment properties. It makes total sense. You eliminate interest payments on the loan borrowed and you eliminate the overhead of the loan itself. My opinion is that your tolerance for risk will determine your approach. High risk equals high returns. I personally have a low tolerance for risk, but then again, I am not interested in real estate investing. For high-risk individuals, you have to weigh your current income against the financial risk associated with the rental property.

If the goal is a stress free retirement, I suggest cash only or majority cash fronted. If the goal is to chase your dream of being a real estate tycoon, you should at a minimum have 30% equity in the property at the time of purchase. This will allow you to only be responsible for 70% of the total loan, and gives you room to sell the property for possible return if trouble comes. We constantly talk about life happening and trouble definitely will come, so you have to plan accordingly even if you are more risk tolerant.

Entrepreneurship

Another option especially for driven individuals is to invest in your own company. Real estate investing is a form of entrepreneurship where you can replace your current income with the income of something you are more passionate about. Maybe you have worked 20 years and have followed every step in this book, but yet, you are still unfulfilled with passion from day to day. Investing in yourself is a great option if you have something you are passionate about.

One of the greatest things about not living paycheck-to-paycheck and being financially free is that you have options as far as income. You have no overhead forcing you to work a certain job. At this point, it is totally low risk to attack your goals of doing what you are passionate about. Not to mention, you do not have to totally replace your current job.

I previously worked with a guy who was an IT (information technology) professional by career title, and owned a private owned vitamin and sports enhancement shop. When he first purchased the shop from the previous owner, he worked countless hours after his IT job creating the culture he wanted his shop to have. After several months of this, he was able to let his managers drive the culture and simply dropped in from time to time. He even invested more into the shop by opening up sales revenue via the Internet.

He definitely had overhead from financing the purchase of the store, but there are tons of other side businesses or full time businesses that do not require a lot of initial financing to start. The key is to try your best to build wealth without the overhead of financing and additional loans. It is doable but takes time and good planning to accomplish.

Writing this book is an entrepreneurship investment for me. Most of it will be a time investment, but we all know time is money. Also, I will have to make additional financial investments to help edit, publish, and market my book in order to get return cash revenue. I also have a side travel business that helps generate additional cash flow. I love travel so it made sense to help others enjoy it as much as I do. I have to pay a fee monthly to be allowed to make commission on my bookings. That monthly fee is my investment into my side business and myself.

If you are really passionate about running your own business, I highly suggest getting your personal finances in line first. If not, you will definitely add a ton of credit risk, which can lead you back to the paycheck-to-paycheck cycle. A lot of entrepreneur advocates will say my previous statement is completely wrong and the time to do what you want is NOW! You jump on the train if you want to, but it is a fact that having your personal finances in line will allow you more flexibility when it comes to building a business. Once they are in line, you have the flexibility to invest in yourself and not rely on credit and financial institutions. These institutions only benefit from the interest your business will pay.

Chapter 6 - Wealth Over Riches' Financial Blueprint

I would like to finish the book by saying thank you for not only taking the time to read my book, but for investing in yourself. I never regret any of the books I have read, for I have gained at least one thing from each book I have read to apply to my life. In this chapter, I will briefly recap the book, but in a blueprint format. This blueprint is not an exact linear projection of my life, but instead a blueprint of what I would do if I could start over. I hope this blueprint can be beneficial to you in some way, and that you continue to strive for financial freedom while building wealth.

Always remember, the road of escaping the paycheck-to-paycheck cycle is not always perfect. You will experience life events that are out of your control, but stick to your overall goal and plan. The blueprint should be used to minimize the effect life events have on your life, but also set the simple principles that lead to wealth. Everyone reading this book will not follow the blueprint and some will deviate a little or utilize certain steps in their path. My goal in writing this book was to help spark financial change, and I hope you utilize the blueprint for your own benefit.

1. Create Budget

You cannot attack your financial problems if you are unaware of them. The budget will help you map out your spending so you know exactly where the money is going.

2. Open Up Cash Flow

Once the budget is in place, you can see what can be cut or reduced to help open up additional cash flow. Remember the top budget line items that can be reduced are housing, transportation, and entertainment.

3. Open Up First Emergency Savings Account

If you have not opened a savings account linked to your checking account, now is the time. Remember this account is your first emergency savings account. You should aim for a minimum $1,000 and a maximum of $5,000.

4. Pay Off Debt

With your first emergency savings account in place, it is now time to attack any debt and rescue yourself from the paycheck-to-paycheck cycle. My suggestion is to use the avalanche method on all debt except your mortgage. This will save you the most money overall. It is key to know that depending on the amount of debt this stage will be the longest. Remember your overall goals and continue to attack the debt and eliminate the overhead.

5. Open Up Second Emergency Savings Account

Once you have escaped the overhead and debt, it is now time to secure your freedom from the paycheck-to-paycheck cycle. A second emergency savings account with three to six months of bills will help prepare you against any life events including losing your main income for sometime. You want to maximize the return on your investment and open a high-yield savings account. High-yield savings accounts have a higher interest payout than typical bank savings accounts.

6. Secure Your Retirement

I highly suggest setting your 401k or retirement accounts before your first paycheck, but for those who do not have those in place already it is time to do so now. You already have no debt besides your mortgage and emergency savings in place; securing your retirement should be your number one priority at this point.

7. Life Insurance and College Savings

After securing your retirement, you want to secure your family's future. If you were to die, would you be leaving a bill or money? This is where a term life insurance policy comes into play. Additionally, you want to set up your kids for their future. Opening up a 529-college savings account is a perfect way to do so.

8. Big Expense Savings

Once you reach saving for your children's college expenses, you are super clear from the previous paycheck-to-paycheck cycle lifestyle. You can now plan accordingly for any near-term purchases such as a car, home improvement, or furniture. You can even invest in yourself and start your side business.

9. Pay Off Mortgage

The last step in financial freedom is alleviating the last debt and financial overhead. This is a big step, and you have to really plan accordingly. You should come up with a plan and attack your mortgage accordingly.

10. Financial Freedom

Once your mortgage is paid off and everything else in the blueprint is accomplished, you are now financially free! Other than transportation, food, taxes, and maybe children expenses, you no longer have any major financial obligations. You are now able to enjoy the peace of financial freedom.

Chapter 7 - Author's Financial Goals

As mentioned countless times in the book, I am here to be as vulnerable as possible while providing what I have learned from my research and readings. There is no other way to wrap up a financial book without being vulnerable and sharing my own personal finance goals and what I am doing to ensure I can reach them. I hope my goals can inspire you to think bigger, and strive for wealth.

As a precursor, I believe it is important to introduce where I am currently in the wealth-building race. As a family, my wife and I acquired two Bachelor's and two Masters' degrees and completely paid off any student loan debt associated with those degrees. We outright own a Toyota Camry and a Jeep Grand Cherokee. We have a small emergency savings account with our local bank, and a bigger emergency savings account with 3-6 months of "needs" bills in a high-yield savings account. We currently have a mortgage north of $200,000, but no other debt. We both have 401k plans with pre-tax allocation matching our company's match. Additionally, we allocate the maximum amount allowed into an HSA account. My wife has a 20-year term life insurance policy. I have life insurance through my employer and pay an additional post-tax fee to extend my life insurance and cover my daughter as well. We have a 529-college savings plan for my only child at the time of writing this. Now, you have a clear picture of where we are financially, and now for our goals.

Short-term Goals

1. Car Purchase Savings

My wife's car has around 150,000 miles on it, and it is the perfect time to start saving for a new one. Will we buy a new one immediately after saving the money? No, but I am practicing the habit of forecasting. She drives the Camry, so the car can probably make it to 250,000-300,000 easily. I am preparing for that day, ahead of schedule, to ensure we have the money at the time that we actually need it. Also, I plan to pay cash for the next vehicle and cap off the purchase at a reasonable price. Again, always avoid financing a car.

2. Travel Savings

I love to travel, and it is actually my desired want. I make sure I have a budget to fund my yearly traveling expenses. So for me, it is needs first followed by a travel budget, which is then followed by savings goals! Since I associate my traveling into my goals, it really is needs then savings followed by my wants.

3. Additional College Savings

I currently have a 3 year old, and I know the time is ticking on the next child. Planning the birth of a child is a huge part of forecasting for your budget. I know pretty soon I will probably be a blessed father of two children. I want to set up all of my children equally to succeed in life; so whenever I am blessed with an additional one, I plan to open up an additional 529-college savings plan.

Long-term Goals

1. Completely Debt Free

With my only debt being my mortgage, my goal is to pay off my mortgage well before its 30-year loan term. The joy of waking up completely debt free sounds marvelous. I literally will walk into work with a different walk. To accomplish this goal, I will split my savings into two buckets. One bucket will be allocated to my high-yield savings account. In that account, I will have my six-month emergency savings, car savings, traveling savings, and any additional short-term goal savings. In the second bucket, I will allocate all the money towards additional mortgage payments. I already know; I can most likely beat my mortgage interest rate by continuing to invest the additional money. For me, the price of paying off my house as soon as possible is greater than having additional money in my portfolio. We have to remember real wealth is built by investing over time, and not what returns you get in a couple months or a year. Once my mortgage is eliminated, I have the option to then save more or leverage to invest in myself or side business.

2. Save for Children's College Education

At a minimum, I want to be able to cover tuition and fees for my children if they decide to attend college. With my current allocations, I am hoping to cover the full price of attending college for them. I already have the steps in place, but continuing to keep the process in place is the overall goal.

3. Purchase International Property

I have no dreams of being a real estate tycoon, but I would love to own a villa in Aruba or another Caribbean island. The key is I want to pay cash for the property. Again, I want to live a debt free life, so I am leaving wealth and not bills after I die.

4. Retire as a Millionaire at 60

At a young age, this might have seemed far fetched; but hopefully after reading this book, you believe it too. I already have a process in place via my 401k allocations. The key is to continue the process by adding more to the process. I currently invest at the percentage that my company matches. After a yearly raise, I will up my investment percentage by the raise percentage. I will continue to do so until I reach the maximum allotted into a 401k. With this plan, I am sure to exceed the one million dollar goals by 60. I am sure I will still have additional income coming in at 60, but my goal is to prepare myself to not to have to work.

References

Collins, J L. The Simple Path to Wealth: Your Road Map to Financial Independence And A Rich, Free Life. North Charleston. CreateSpace Independent Publishing Platform, 2016.

Ramsey, Dave. The Total Money Makeover: A Proven Plan for Financial Fitness. Nashville: Nelson Books, 2007.

Trench, Scott. Set for Life: Dominate Life, Money, and the American Dream. Denver. BiggerPockets, 2017.

Made in the USA
Columbia, SC
08 January 2020